〈개정판〉

비전공자를 위한

안드로이드 앱 프로그래밍

정민포·조혁규 共著

 21세기사

이 도서의 국립중앙도서관 출판예정도서목록(CIP)은 서지정보유통지원시스템 홈페이지(http://seoji.nl.go.kr)와 국가자료공동목록시스템 (http://www.nl.go.kr/kolisnet)에서 이용하실 수 있습니다.(CIP제어번호: CIP2018006530)

F•O•R•E•W•O•R•D

제4차 산업혁명은 2017년 현재 진행하고 있으며, 이미 사회 곳곳에 그 현상이 드러나고 있습니다. 전 세계적으로 10억명 이상의 실업자가 있으며, 이미 많은 일자리가 사라졌고, 앞으로도 더 많이 사라질 것이라고 예상됩니다. 연구결과에 따라 다르지만, 현재보다 80~99%의 일자리가 사라진다고 예상하고 있습니다. 하지만, 사라지는 일자리만큼 새로운 신규 일자리도 만들어지고 있습니다. 유망한 분야로는 로봇, 인공지능, 나노, 3D 프린터, IoT, 핀테크, 드론, 자율주행, 가상현실+증강현실, 블록체인, 빅데이터 사이버펑크, 양자컴퓨터, 정보보호 등이 있습니다. 이러한 배경으로 공학, 자연, 인문, 사회 계열 등과 관련된 대학 및 산업분야에서는 기존 교육에 S/W를 활용한 제품 개발, 서비스 및 혁신 등이 요구됩니다.

2017년 1월에 개설된 영산대학교 S/W교육센터는 이러한 추세에 맞추어 다양한 S/W 교육을 시행합니다. 관련 전공 대상자에게는 체계적인 S/W교육을, 영산대학교 전체 학생들에게는 S/W기초교육과 S/W심화교육을, 대학 주변의 초,중,고 및 일반인과 공무원 등에게는 S/W 가치확산을 위한 다양한 교양 S/W 교육을 실시하고 있습니다. 개발된 교재는 2017년 1학기, 2학기에 걸쳐 1년 동안 비전공자들을 대상으로 한 앱 교육을 한 내용입니다. 비전공학생들이 처음 교육을 받을 때는 많은 저항이 있었습니다. "어떻게 우리가 IT 전공학생들이 배우는 코딩을 배울 수가 있는가! 우리는 할 수 없다!" 등의 저항이었습니다. 하지만 시간이 흐를수록, 전공교육 과정에 포함되어 운영되는 교육과정이라 조금씩 적응하기 시작하였습니다. 2학기를 마감하는 지금은 대부분의 학생들이 앱을 어려워하지만, 이제는 스스럼없이 자신의 아이디어를 직접 제작해보기 시작했습니다. IT 전공자처럼 자바 문법을 모두 배우고 앱을 개발할 수는 없었습니다. 본 교재에는 포함되어 있지 않지만 필요한 자바 문법은 조금씩 앱에 포함시켜 교육을 하였습니다. 앞으로 1년 정도 더 학생들이 이 분야에 조금 더 노력을 한다면, 자신의 전공에 IT 분야를 접목할 수 있는 인력으로 성장할 것으로 기대합니다.

지난 1년간 IT 전공이 아닌 학생들에게 앱 개발에 관한 교육을 담당하면서 학생들의 어려움과 가르치는 사람의 어려움이 많은 것을 보고 느꼈기에 서로의 어려움에 도움을 줄 수 없을까 하는 고민이 있었습니다. 이 책은 비전공자이면서 앱 교육에 참여한 학생들에게 실질적으로 도움이 되도록 구성하였으며, 진행되는 주제에 따라서 구성하였습니다. 각 장의 내용을 잘 따라서 진행하면 더욱 큰 교육 효과를 기대할 수 있을 것으로 생각하여, 비전공자로 앱 프로그래밍을 공부하면서 어려움에 봉착한 학생들에게 기댈 수 있는 하나의 버팀목 역할을 할 수 있기를 희망합니다.

2017년 초겨울 천성산 기슭에서...

C • O • N • T • E • N • T • S

안드로이드 개요와 환경 구축

안드로이드의 역사

학습목표

안드로이드 운영체제의 역사를 알 수 있다.

위키백과에서는 안드로이드(운영체제)를 다음과 같이 정의하고 있다[1].

> 안드로이드(영어: Android)는 휴대 전화를 비롯한 휴대용 장치를 위한 운영 체제와 미들웨어, 사용자 인터페이스 그리고 표준 응용 프로그램(웹 브라우저, 이메일 클라이언트, 단문 메시지 서비스(SMS), 멀티미디어 메시지 서비스(MMS)등)을 포함하고 있는 소프트웨어 스택이자 **모바일 운영 체제**이다.
>
> 안드로이드는 개발자들이 **자바 언어로 응용 프로그램을 작성할 수 있게** 하였으며, 컴파일된 바이트코드를 구동할 수 있는 런타임 라이브러리를 제공한다. 또한 안드로이드 소프트웨어 개발 키트(SDK)를 통해 응용 프로그램을 개발하는 데 필요한 각종 도구와 API를 제공한다.
>
> 안드로이드는 **리눅스 커널 위에서 동작**하며, 다양한 안드로이드 시스템 구성 요소에서 사용되는 C/C++ 라이브러리들을 포함하고 있다. 안드로이드는 기존의 자바 가상 머신과는 다른 가상 머신인 달빅 가상 머신을 통해 자바로 작성된 응용 프로그램을 별도의 프로세스에서 실행하는 구조로 되어 있다.

2005년 7월 :
- 구글은 미국 캘리포니아 주의 팔로알토에 위치한 작은 안드로이드사를 인수
- 안드로이드사는 앤디 루빈이 세운 업체

2007년 11월 5일 :
- 텍사스 인스트루먼트, 브로드컴 코퍼레이션, 구글, HTC, 인텔, LG전자, 마벨 테크놀로지 그룹, 모토로라, 엔비디아, 퀄컴, 삼성전자, 스프린트 넥스텔, T-모바일의 몇몇 회사로 구성된 컨소시엄인 오픈 핸드셋 얼라이언스(OHA)가 모바일 기기의 공개 표준을 개발하는 것을 목표로 결성
- OHA는 리눅스 커널 2.6에서 빌드된 그들의 첫 번째 모바일 기기 플랫폼 결과물인 안드로이드를 발표

2008년 10월 21일 :
- 안드로이드가 오픈 소스로 선언
- 구글은 네트워크와 텔레폰 스택을 포함하는 완전한 소스 코드를 아파치 라이선스로 공개

2008년 12월 9일 :
- ARM 홀딩스, 아세로스(Atheros Communications), 에이수스, 가르민, 소프트뱅크, 소니 에릭슨, 도시바, 보다폰으로 구성된 새로운 14개의 멤버가 안드로이드 프로젝트에 참여

2013년 12월 12일 :
- 현재 API만 완전한 공개 소스인 상태이며 VM에 대한 소스는 공개하지 않음
- 그런 점에서 완전한 오픈소스 스마트폰 운영체제라고 할 수는 없음

안드로이드는 구글에 의해 개발 되고 있으며 현재(2017.11.18.)의 안드로이드 버전 히스토리는 다음과 같다[1][2].

버전 이름은 알파벳 C부터 알파벳순으로 이어갔다.

1.0에서는 A부터 알파벳순으로 로봇의 이름을 붙이려 Astro Boy라는 이름을 내부에서 붙였고 1.1에서는 이 규칙을 위반한 채 디저트가 좋다는 PM의 취향으로 Petit Four으로 지정하였다. 1.5 버전부터 지금의 체제를 완성했다. Astro Boy는 공식적인 이름으로 인정받지는 못했다.

코드명	버전	특징
Cupcake (컵케이크)	1.5 API Level 3	동영상 녹화와 블루투스 A2DP, AVRCP 지원 한국어 추가 Linux Kernel : 2.6.27
Donut (도넛)	1.6 API Level 4	다중 선택/삭제 지원 WVGA화면 해상도 지원 CDMA, EVDO, 802.1x 등의 기술 지원 Linux Kernel : 2.6.29
Éclair (이클레어)	2.0 API Level 5 2.0.1 API Level 6 2.1 API Level 7	HTML5 지원 마이크로소프트 익스체이지 지원 카메라 내장 플래시 지원 블루투스 2.1 개선된 가상 키보드 Linux Kernel : 2.6.29
Froyo (프로요(프로즌 요거트))	2.2 API Level 8 2.2.1 API Level 8 2.2.2 API Level 8	OS 속도 개선 및 Adobe Flash 10.1지원 크롬이 V8 자바스크립트 엔진 지원 USB 테더링 및 와이파이 핫스팟 기능 지원 자동 업데이트 기능 지원 확장 메모리에 응용 프로그램 설치 지원 Linux Kernel : 2.6.32
Gingerbread (진저브레드)	2.3~2.3.2 API Level 9 2.3.3~2.3.7 API Level 10	인터넷 전화 및 NFC 지원 자이로스코프, 회전 벡터, 기압계 등 지원 OpenSL ES 구현 제공 Linux Kernel : 2.6.35

코드명	버전	특징
Honeycomb (허니콤)	3.0 API Level 11 3.1 API Level 12 3.2 API Level 13	태블릿 PC에 최적화된 UI 지원 개선된 멀티 태스킹 기능 USB 액세서리 연결 마이크로 SD 지원 기능 조이스틱과 게임패드 지원 Linux Kernel : 2.6.36
Ice Cream Sandwich (아이스크림 샌드위치)	4.0~4.0.2 API Level 14 4.0.3~4.0.4 API Level 15	안드로이드 빔 지원 카메라 성능 향상 Version 4.0~4.0.1 Linux Kernel : 3.0.1 Version 4.0.3~4.0.4 Linux Kernel : 3.0.8
Jellybean (젤리빈)	4.1~4.1.2 API Level 16	HTML5와 자바스크립트 성능 향상 구글크롬이 기본 브라우저 Linux Kernel : 3.0.31
	4.2~4.2.2 API Level 17	SeLinux 무선 디스플레이(미라캐스트) 세계시간을 탑재한 새로운 시계 앱 Linux Kernel : 3.0.53
	4.3~4.3.1 API Level 18	블루투스 LE와 오픈GL ES 3.0 지원 오아피파이 성능 및 사용시 편의성 개선 Linux Kernel : 3.4.0
Kitkat (킷캣)	4.4~4.4.4 API Level 19	달빅 캐시 정리 등 메모리 관리 기능 GPU 가속 클라우드 프린팅 지원 SELinux 보안 강화 Linux Kernel : 3.4
Lollipop (롤리팝)	5.0~5.0.2 API Level 21 5.1.0~5.1.1 API Level 22	달빅 캐시를 ART로 완전 변경 64비트 CPU 정식 지원 OpenGL ES 3.1 지원 HD보이스 지원 Linux Kernel : 3.4
Marshmallow (마시멜로)	6.0~6.0.1 API Level 23	런타임 권한 잠자기 및 앱 디기모드 절전 기능 Linux Kernel : 3.10.83

코드명	버전	특징
Nougat (누가)	7.0 API Level 24 7.1 API Level 25	다중창 지원 알림 향상프로필 가이드 방식의 JIT/AOT 잠자기 모드 Linux Kernel : 4.7.2
Oreo (오레오)	8.0 API Level 26	부팅 속도 2배 향상 백그라운드 앱 활동성 최소화 앱 로그인 자동화 픽처 인 픽처(PIP)를 통한 2개의 앱 동시 실행 알림 닷이 새 소식을 빠르게 보여줌 구글 플레이 프로텍트 배터리 성능 향상 Linux Kernel : X

JAVA 환경 구축

JAVA 환경을 설정할 수 있다.

안드로이드 앱을 개발하기 위한 운영체제는 Windows, Linux, Mac을 사용할 수 있다. 대부분의 사용자가 Windows 환경을 사용하기 때문에, 교재에서는 Windows 환경에서 앱을 개발하는 환경을 소개한다.

안드로이드 앱은 JAVA 언어를 기반으로 만들어지기 때문에 사용자의 PC에 JAVA 개발자 버전을 설치해야 한다.

먼저 JAVA를 설치하기 위한 설치 파일을 ORACLE 홈페이지(http://www.oracle.com/technetwork/java/javase/downloads/index.html?ssSourceSiteId=ocomen)에서 다운로드 한다.

[그림 1-1]과 같이 JDK를 메뉴를 선택한다.

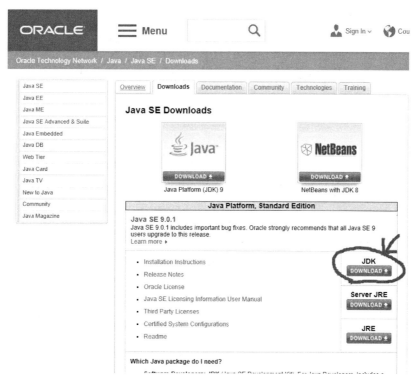

[그림 1-1] ORACLE 홈페이지에서 JDK 선택

[그림 1-2]와 같이 Java SE Development Kit 9.0.1을 다운받기 위해 동의 버튼을 선택한다.

Java SE Development Kit 9.0.1

You must accept the Oracle Binary Code License Agreement for Java SE to download this software.

○ Accept License Agreement   ◉ Decline License Agreement

Product / File Description	File Size	Download
Linux	304.99 MB	⬇jdk-9.0.1_linux-x64_bin.rpm
Linux	338.11 MB	⬇jdk-9.0.1_linux-x64_bin.tar.gz
macOS	382.11 MB	⬇jdk-9.0.1_osx-x64_bin.dmg
Windows	375.51 MB	⬇jdk-9.0.1_windows-x64_bin.exe
Solaris SPARC	206.85 MB	⬇jdk-9.0.1_solaris-sparcv9_bin.tar.gz

[그림 1-2] Java SE Development Kit 9.0.1 다운로드 동의하기

동의 버튼을 선택하면, [그림 1-3]과 같이 화면이 변경된다. [그림1-3]에서 Windows를 선택한다. 필자의 운영체제는 Windows10이고 64bit OS이기 때문에 자동으로 jdk-9.0.1_windows-x64_bin.exe가 화면에 나온다. 만약 32bit OS라면 32bit 버전의 jdk가 자동으로 보이게 된다.

Java SE Development Kit 9.0.1

You must accept the Oracle Binary Code License Agreement for Java SE to download this software.
Thank you for accepting the Oracle Binary Code License Agreement for Java SE; you may now download this software.

Product / File Description	File Size	Download
Linux	304.99 MB	⬇jdk-9.0.1_linux-x64_bin.rpm
Linux	338.11 MB	⬇jdk-9.0.1_linux-x64_bin.tar.gz
macOS	382.11 MB	⬇jdk-9.0.1_osx-x64_bin.dmg
Windows	375.51 MB	⬇jdk-9.0.1_windows-x64_bin.exe
Solaris SPARC	206.85 MB	⬇jdk-9.0.1_solaris-sparcv9_bin.tar.gz

[그림 1-3] 동의를 선택한 후의 화면

jdk-9.0.1_windows-x64_bin.exe를 선택하면 [그림 1-4]처럼 다운 받는 화면이 나온다. "실행"은 바로 설치파일이 실행되는 것이고 저장이나 저장 옆의 아랫 화살표를 누르면 원하는 폴더에 파일을 다운로드 후, 실행하면 설치할 수 있다.

[그림 1-4] Java 설치파일 다운 받기 화면

jdk-9.0.1_windows-x64.bin.exe를 실행하면 [그림1-5]와 같이 설치 화면이 나온다.
"Next〉" 버튼을 선택하여 다음 화면으로 넘어간다.

[그림 1-5] JAVA 설치 화면

[그림 1-6] 설치 화면은 JAVA를 c:\Program Files\Java\jdk-9.0.1\에 설치하는 것을 알
려주고 있다. 사용자가 원하면 이 폴더의 위치를 "Change" 버튼을 선택하여 변경할 수 있
다. 환경 설정에 필요한 변수이기 때문에, 반드시 알고 있어야 한다. 그리고
Development Tools, Source Code, Public JRE는 모두 선택된 상태이기 때문에 그대로 두
고 "Next" 버튼을 선택한다.

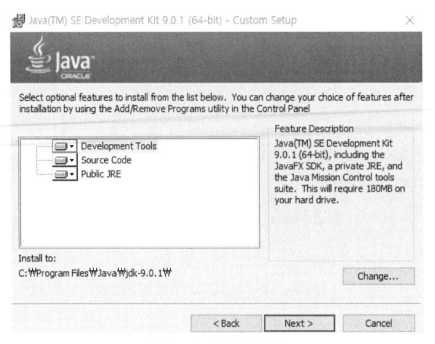

[그림 1-6] JAVA 설치 화면

설치 도중에 [그림 1-7]과 같은 화면이 나오면 "다음" 버튼을 선택한다.

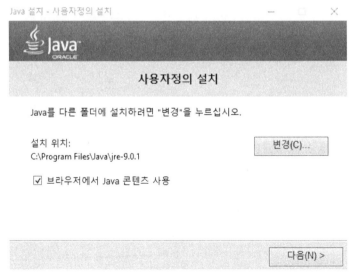

[그림 1-7] 자바 설치 화면

JAVA 설치가 완료되면 [그림 1-8]과 같은 화면이 보인다.

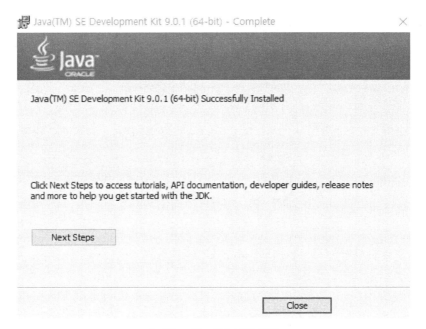

[그림 1-8] 자바 설치 화면

[그림 1-8]의 "Close" 버튼을 선택하면 JAVA 설치는 완료가 된다. 다음 과정은 코드로 개발되는 안드로이드 소스코드를 기계어로 바꾸어주는 컴파일 과정을 수행하기 위해 설치된 자바 환경을 설정한다.

윈도우즈의 버전에 따라 "고급시스템 설정" 메뉴의 위치가 조금씩 다르다는 것을 기억하자. [그림 1-9]에서 "고급시스템 설정" 메뉴를 선택하자.

[그림 1-9] 고급시스템 설정 선택

[그림 1-10]에서 "환경 변수" 메뉴를 선택하자.

[그림 1-10] 환경 변수 메뉴 선택하기

[그림 1-11]에서 "시스템변수" 영역에서 "JAVA_HOME" 변수가 존재하면 "JAVA_HOME" 변수를 선택 후 편집을 누르거나, 만약 변수가 존재하지 않으면 "새로 만들기" 변수를 선택한다. 선택 후에, 그림처럼 변수 이름과 변수 값을 입력하는 창에 다음과 같이 입력한다. 변수 이름에는 JAVA_HOME, 변수 값에는 앞에서 설치한 자바설치 폴더이름을 입력한다. 현재는 C:₩Programfiles₩Java₩jdk-9.0.1을 입력한다. 아래의 "디렉터리 찾아보기"를 통해 JAVA가 설치된 폴더를 찾아가서 선택하는 것을 추천한다. "JAVA_HOME" 변수는 안드로이드 개발 환경인 Android Studio에게 JAVA가 설치된 폴더를 알려준다.

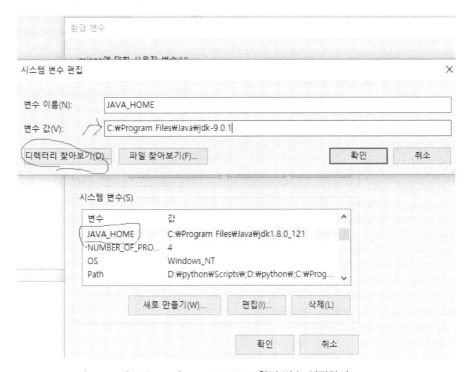

[그림 1-11] JAVA_HOME 환경 변수 설정하기

[그림 1-12]는 JAVA_HOME 환경 변수에 대한 설정 완료 화면이다.

[그림 1-12] JAVA_HOME 환경 변수 설정 완료

다음은 환경변수 "PATH"를 설정해야 한다. 이 환경 변수는 Java 소스 코드를 기계어 코드로 번역해주기 위해 필요한 Java.exe, Javac.exe를 임의의 위치에서 호출할 수 있게 해주는 역할을 한다. [그림 1-13]을 참고하여, Path 선택, Javac.exe, Java.exe가 위치한 "c:₩program files₩java₩jdk-9.0.1₩bin"을 선택한다.

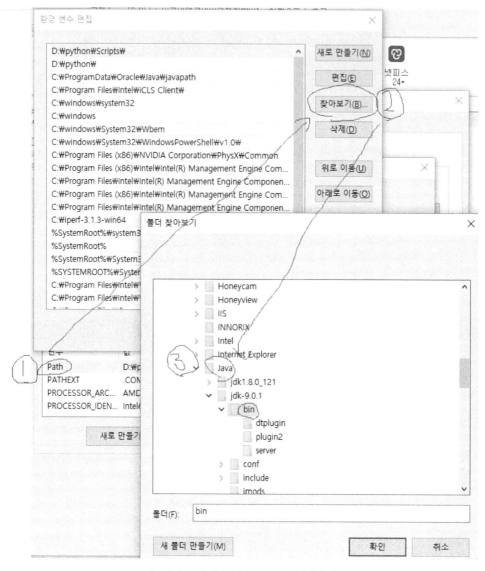

[그림 1-13] PATH 환경 변수 설정하기

[그림 1-14]처럼 PATH가 "c:₩program files₩java₩jdk-9.0.1₩bin"으로 설정된다.

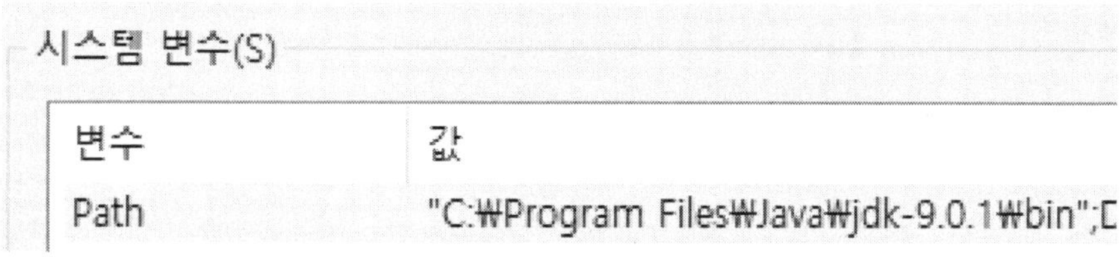

시스템 변수(S)	
변수	값
Path	"C:₩Program Files₩Java₩jdk-9.0.1₩bin";C

[그림 1-14] PATH 환경 설정 결과

[그림 1-15]처럼 PATH가 잘 설치되었는지 확인을 해보자. "명령 프롬프트(도스창)"을 실행시켜 "java -version"을 입력해보자. 아래의 그림처럼 "java version 9.0.1"이 출력되면 환경설정이 완료된 것이다.

■ 명령 프롬프트

```
Microsoft Windows [Version 10.0.14393]
(c) 2016 Microsoft Corporation. All rights reserved.

C:₩Users₩minpo>java -version
java version "9.0.1"
Java(TM) SE Runtime Environment (build 9.0.1+11)
Java HotSpot(TM) 64-Bit Server VM (build 9.0.1+11, mixed mode)

C:₩Users₩minpo>
```

[그림 1-15] java -version으로 설치확인

다음은 "CLASSPATH" 변수를 설정한다. 이 변수는 Java 소스코드를 기계어로 바꾸어 줄 때 필요한 라이브러리(미리 만들어 둔 필요한 기능 모임)가 존재하는 위치를 지정한다. [그림 1-16]에서처럼 환경변수를 설정한다. "디렉토리 찾아보기" 메뉴에서 "c:₩program files₩java₩jdk-9.0.1₩lib"를 찾아 선택한다.

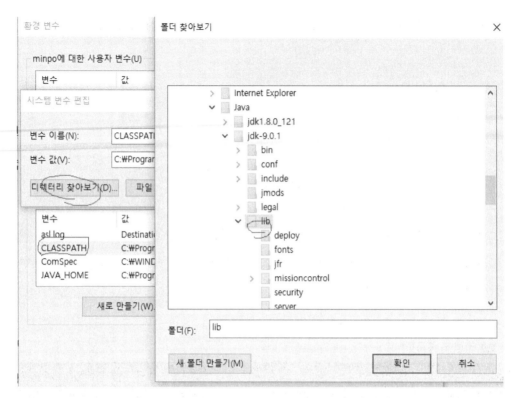

[그림 1-16] CLASSPATH 지정하기

[그림 1-17]은 CLASSPATH 환경변수에 대한 설정 완료 화면이다.

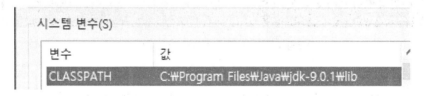

[그림 1-17] CLASSPATH 환경변수 설정 완료 화면

1.3 안드로이드 앱 개발 환경 구축(Android Studio)

학습목표

Android Studio를 설치할 수 있다.

안드로이드 앱 개발 도구인 Android Studio를 설치하기 전에, 1-2절에서 JAVA 설치가 완료되어야 한다.

[그림 1-18]처럼 안드로이드 앱 개발 도구를 https://developer.android.com/studio/index.html 사이트에서 다운로드를 해보자.

[그림 1-18] Android Studio를 다운 받기

[그림 1-19]처럼 android-studio-ide-171.44083382-windows.exe를 다운 받습니다.

플랫폼	Android Studio 패키지	크기	SHA-256 체크섬
Windows (64비트)	android-studio-ide-171.4408382-windows.exe Android SDK 없음	681 MB (714,340,664 bytes)	627d7f346bf4825
	android-studio-ide-171.4408382-windows.zip Android SDK 없음, 설치 프로그램 없음	737 MB (772,863,352 bytes)	7a9ef037e34add6
Windows (32비트)	android-studio-ide-171.4408382-windows32.zip Android SDK 없음, 설치 프로그램 없음	736 MB (772,333,606 bytes)	29399953024b0b
Mac	android-studio-ide-171.4408382-mac.dmg	731 MB (766,935,438 bytes)	f6c455fb1778b39
Linux	android-studio-ide-171.4408382-linux.zip	735 MB (771,324,214 bytes)	7991f95ea1b6c55

[그림 1-19] 안드로이드 설치파일 다운받기

Android 설치파일은 용량이 매우 큽니다. 미리 하드 디스크에 충분한 용량(10G이상)을 확보 바랍니다.

다운로드 받은 파일을 실행하면, [그림 1-20]와 같은 화면이 실행된다.

[그림 1-20] 안드로이드 설치

[그림 1-21]은 Android Studio를 실행하기 위해 필요한 설치 파일을 선택하는 화면이다.
모두 체크해준다.

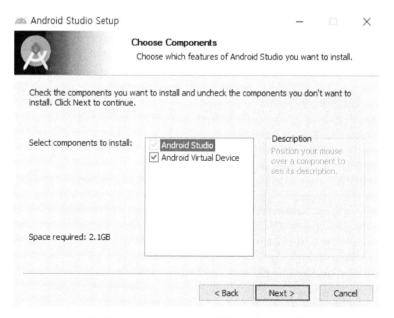

[그림 1-21] 안드로이드 설치(구성요소 설치)

[그림 1-22]는 Android Studio 프로그램이 설치될 폴더를 지정하는 화면이다. 기본 설정 폴더 위치는 "C:₩Program Files₩Android₩Android Studio"이다. 여유가 많은 하드디스크(C:, D:)로 선택하는 것을 추천한다.

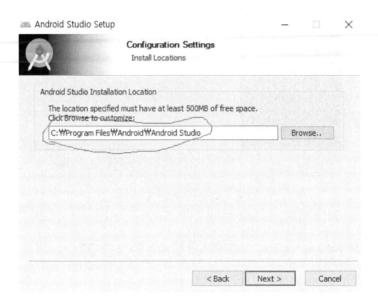

[그림 1-22] 안드로이드 설치(설치 위치 결정)

[그림 1-23]은 설치 완료 화면이다. PC의 성능에 따라 설치시간이 결정된다.

[그림 1-23] 안드로이드 설치 완료

[그림 1-23]에서 "Finish" 버튼을 눌러 Android Studio를 실행한다.

Android Studio를 처음 실행하면 추가 환경 설정을 위해 [그림 1-24]와 같은 화면이 실행
된다.

[그림 1-24] 안드로이드 실행 (추가 환경 설정)

[그림 1-25]에서 두 가지 타입(Standard, Custom)의 설치 타입을 선택할 수 있다.
Standard type은 대부분의 설정을 시스템이 자동으로 해준다. 여기에서는 사용자가 직접
선택사항을 선택하는 Custom Type을 선택한다.

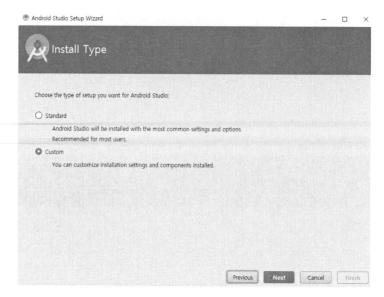

[그림 1-25] 안드로이드 실행(설치 타입 선택)

[그림 1-26]은 Android Studio의 환경 테마를 선택할 수 있다. InteliJ와 Darcula를 선택할 수 있다.

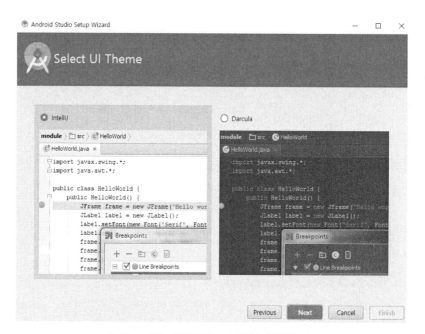

[그림 1-26] 안드로이드 실행(UI 선택하기)

[그림 1-27]은 설치과정에서 매우 중요하다. 안드로이드 앱을 개발하기 위한 개발 도구와 라이브러리를 포함하는 Android SDK와 Android SDK Platform과 안드로이드 앱이 실행되기 위한 가짜 휴대폰(에뮬레이터)인 Android Virtual Device를 설치하는 단계이다. 그리고 SDK가 설치될 위치를 지정한다. 이 위치의 하드디스크는 용량이 충분히 커야 한다. 기본 위치는 "C:₩Users₩minpo₩AppData₩Local₩Android₩Sdk"이다. 이 위치를 꼭 기억하기를 바란다.

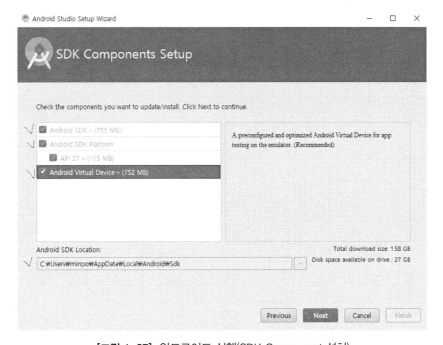

[그림 1-27] 안드로이드 실행(SDK Component 설치)

[그림 1-28]은 안드로이드 환경설정 마지막 과정이다. 마지막으로 SDK가 설치되는 위치와 설정에 필요한 다운로드 사이즈를 확인하자. 이제 "Finish" 버튼을 선택하자.

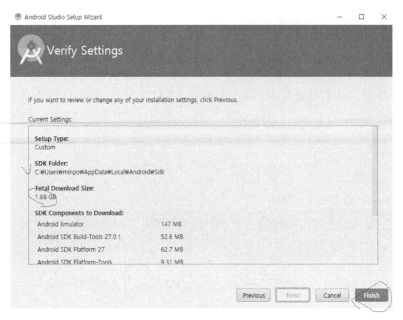

[그림 1-28] 안드로이드 실행(설정 완료)

"Finish" 버튼을 선택하면, 환경 설정에 필요한 다운로드 사이즈(예: 1.68G) 만큼 인터넷
으로부터 다운로드 한다. 네트워크 환경에 따라 시간이 오래 걸릴 수 있다.

[그림 1-29]는 모든 환경 설정이 끝나고 실행되는 Android Studio의 첫 화면이다.

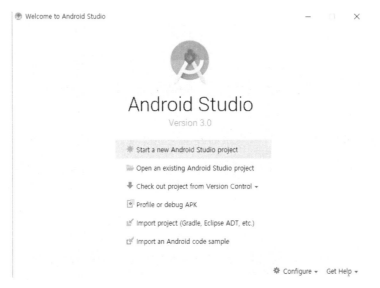

[그림 29] Android Studio 프로그램의 첫 화면

참·고·자·료

[1]   안드로이드 운영체제의 정의, 위키피디아(https://ko.wikipedia.org/wiki)

[2]   안드로이드 개발자 사이트, https://developer.android.com/guide/topics/
       manifest/uses-sdk-element.html#ApiLevels

Android Studio로 첫 프로그램 만들어보기

아마도 이 책을 읽는 비전공자는 "프로그램 경험도 없고 컴퓨터도 잘 모르는데 어떻게 프로그램을 바로 할 수 있을까?"라는 의구심을 가질 것이다. 프로그램을 처음하는 비전공자에게 저자가 추천하는 방법은 "무 조건 따라 해보세요! 그래야 관심을 가질 수 있습니다!"

다음의 "Hello!!! Wise You!" 프로그램을 직접 따라해 보고, 실행하는 방법을 알게 되면 프로그램에 대해 처음과 다른 조금 다른 자세를 가질 것이라 확신합니다.

2.1 "Hello!!! Wise You!" 프로그램 만들기

학습목표

안드로이드 첫 프로그램을 만들 수 있다.

안드로이드 앱을 만들기 위해, 개발도구인 Android Studio를 실행하기 위해 [그림 2-1]과
같이 메뉴를 찾아 "Android Studio"를 실행합니다.

[그림 2-1] Android Studio 메뉴

[그림 2-2]처럼 Android Studio의 첫 화면이 실행됩니다. 첫 화면 실행 후, "Start a new Android Studio project"를 선택합니다.

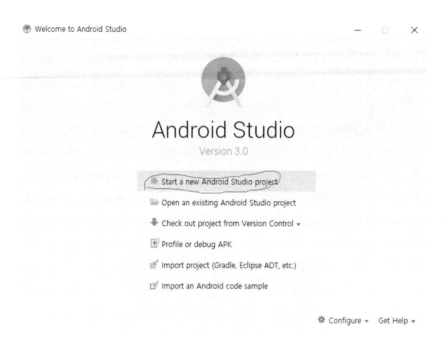

[그림 2-2] Android Studio 프로그램의 첫 화면

[그림 2-3]은 새로운 Android Project를 만들기 위한 환경 설정 단계입니다. Application Name에 Hello! Wise You!를 입력합니다. Company domain에는 Google Play에 앱을 등록할 때 필요합니다. Project location은 개발되는 앱의 저장 위치입니다.

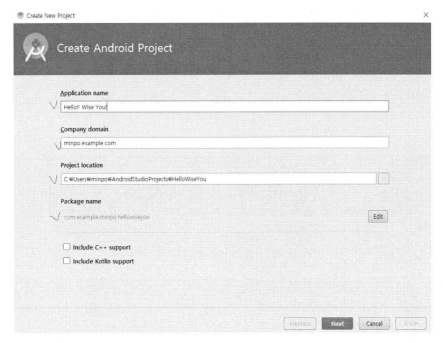

[그림 2-3] Android Project 환경 설정

이전 버전에서 보이지 않던 "Include Kotlin support"가 있습니다. Kotlin(코틀린)을 간략히 소개하면 다음과 같습니다[1].

> 코틀린 (Kotlin)은 Scala등과 같이 자바가상머신(JVM) 언어에서 돌아가는 Jetbrains에서 만든 개발언어 이다. 다시말하자면, Kotlin을 컴파일 하면 JVM에서 돌아가는 bytecode를 생성해준다. Jetbrain은 요즘 개발자 사이에서 커다란 인기를 끌고있는 IntelliJ 시리즈 (Java, Python, Ruby, C, Javascript 등등 언어별 각각의 최적의 IDE를 제공)로 유명한 회사이고 최근에는 Android Studio 가 Jebrains의 IDE 플랫폼으로 제작되어 더욱 많이 알려졌다. 따라서 일단 Kotlin을 쓸때 IDE 걱정은 할필요 없다는 것이 첫번째 장점이다.

당장은 관심을 가지지 않아도 되나, 개발자라면 관심을 가져야 합니다.

[그림 2-4]는 개발되는 안드로이드 프로그램이 최소 어떤 버전의 운영체제에서 작동될 것인
가와 어떤 디바이스(Phone, Wear, TV 등)에서 실행될 것인가를 결정하는 메뉴입니다. 예제
에서는 API 15 버전을 선택했습니다. (1장에서 API 15버전이 무엇인지 확인 바랍니다.)
API 15 버전 이상에서만 개발된 앱이 실행될 수 있다는 의미입니다.

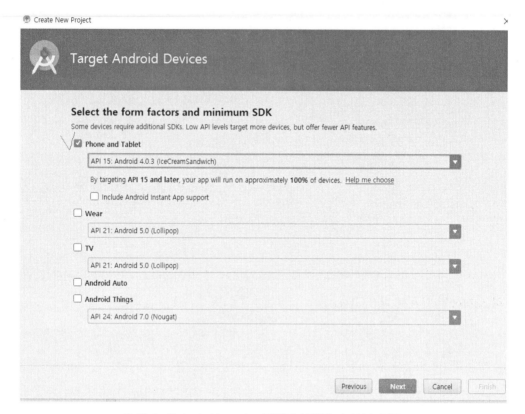

[그림 2-4] Android version 결정과 실행될 디바이스 결정

[그림 2-5]에서 보이는 것처럼 디바이스에 설치된 Android 운영체제별 통계[2]를 확인해
보면, 안드로이드 앱을 개발할 때 최소 버전을 무엇으로 할지 결정할 수 있습니다. API 15
버전은 전체 안드로이드 디바이스의 0.5%만 사용하고 있습니다. 현재는 6.0 Version인
마쉬멜로(API 23)가 30.9%로 가장 많이 사용하고 있습니다.

Version	Codename	API	Distribution
2.3.3 - 2.3.7	Gingerbread	10	0.5%
4.0.3 - 4.0.4	Ice Cream Sandwich	15	0.5%
4.1.x	Jelly Bean	16	2.2%
4.2.x		17	3.1%
4.3		18	0.9%
4.4	KitKat	19	13.8%
5.0	Lollipop	21	6.4%
5.1		22	20.8%
6.0	Marshmallow	23	30.9%
7.0	Nougat	24	17.6%
7.1		25	3.0%
8.0	Oreo	26	0.3%

2017년 11월 9일까지 7일 동안 수집된 데이터
배포율이 0.1% 이하인 버전은 표시되지 않습니다.

[그림 2-5] Android version 통계

[그림 2-6]에서는 개발되는 프로그램의 첫 화면을 무엇으로 할지 결정하는 메뉴입니다. "Empty Activity"는 빈 화면을 의미합니다. 즉, 화면에 아무 것도 없다는 의미입니다.

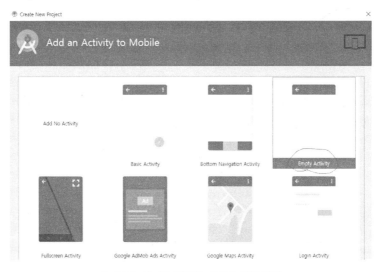

[그림 2-6] 첫 화면(Activity) 선택하기

[그림 2-7]은 Activity Name을 "MainActivity", Layout Name을 "activity_main"으로 지정하는 화면입니다. Layout Name인 "activity_main.xml"은 안드로이드 화면에 나타날 여러 가지 위젯(Widget, 버튼, 그림 등)의 정보를 저장하는 파일입니다. Activity Name인 "MainActivity.java"는 화면에 나타난 버튼 등의 다양한 위젯에 대한 행동을 정의하는 코드를 저장하는 파일입니다.

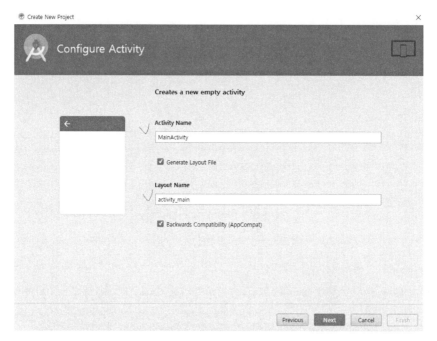

[그림 2-7] Activity Name과 Layout Name 결정하기

일부 시스템에서는 [그림 2-8]과 같은 오류가 발생할 수도 있습니다. 만약 오류가 발생하면 오류 메시지에서 요구하는 대로 처리해야 합니다. [그림 2-8]의 경우에는 "Install missing platform(s) and sync project" 오류가 발생하였습니다.

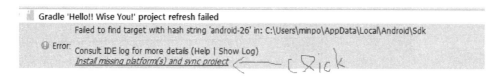

[그림 2-8] 안드로이드 앱 프로젝트 오류 발생(Install missing...)

이 경우, 그 메시지를 선택하면 [그림 2-9]와 같은 화면이 나옵니다. 이 메시지는 안드로이드 앱을 실행하기 위한 환경이 설치 미완료의 의미입니다.

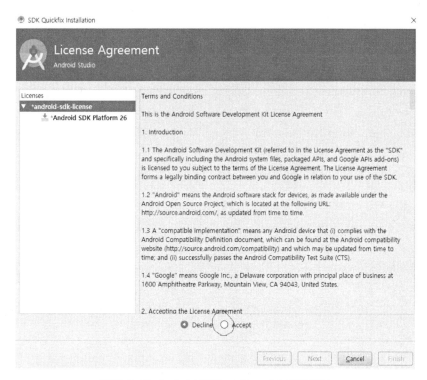

[그림 2-9] Android SDK platform 26 설치 화면

[그림 2-9] 화면에서 "Accept"를 선택하고 "Next" 버튼을 선택합니다. [2-10] 화면에서 필요한 Android SDK를 다운로드하고 있습니다. 완료 후에 "Finish" 버튼을 누릅니다.

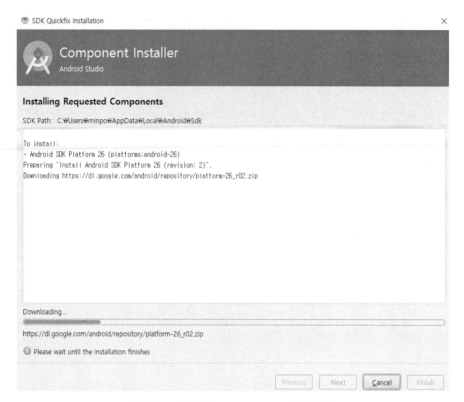

[그림 2-10] 추가 Android SDK 설치 화면

설치가 끝난 뒤에, 또 다른 오류 "Install Build Tools 26.0.2 and sync project"가 발생합니다. 이런 종류의 오류가 발생하면 앞의 과정과 마찬가지로 반복 실행합니다.

안드로이드 프로그램을 개발할 때, 주의할 점은 [그림 2-11]처럼 Android Studio의 작업 표시줄(맨 아래)에 "2 process running..."이라는 메시지가 표시되고 있다면, Andorid Studio가 현재 코드를 기계어로 변경하는 작업을 하고 있다는 뜻입니다. 그 메시지가 표시되는 동안, 메시지가 사라질 때까지 개발자는 기다려야 합니다.

[그림 2-11] Android Studio 작업 중을 의미하는 화면

Android Studio의 작업 메시지가 사라진 후에 [그림 2-12]와 같이 코딩 작업을 할 수 있는 화면이 생성됩니다.

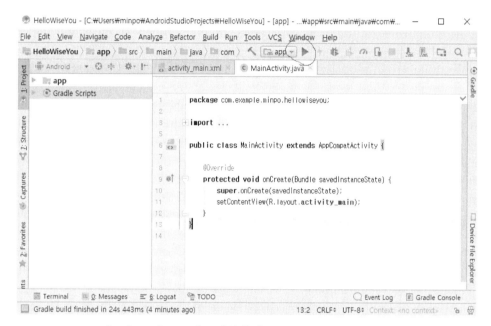

[그림 2-12] 프로젝트 생성 후의 Android Studio 개발 환경

[그림 2-12]에서 표시된 실행 버튼(▶)을 선택합니다. 이 버튼은 시스템 내의 가짜휴대폰 (에뮬레이터)에서 개발된 안드로이드 앱을 실행합니다.

[그림 2-13]에서 개발된 앱을 어떤 디바이스(Target)에서 실행할지 선택합니다. "Nexus 5X API 27 x86"을 선택합니다.

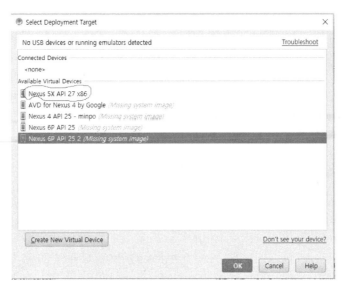

[그림 2-13] Virtual Device 선택 (가짜 휴대폰)

만약 새로운 디바이스(가짜 휴대폰)을 만들고 싶다면 "Create New Virtual Device" 버튼을 선택합니다. [그림 2-14]에서 Virtual Device를 선택합니다. 새로 업데이트 된 구글의 "Pixel XL" 폰을 선택합니다.

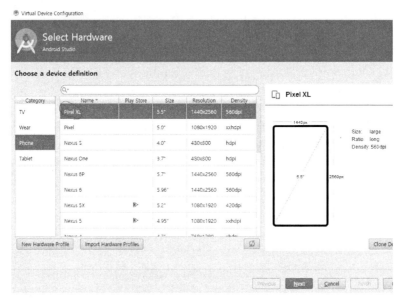

[그림 2-14] 새로운 Virtual Device 선택

[그림 2-15]에서는 Virtual Device(가짜 휴대폰)에서 실행될 안드로이드 운영체제를 선택
합니다. 이미 "API 27"이 설치되어 있기 때문에 "API 27"을 선택합니다.
다른 최신 버전을 선택하고 싶으면 Download(예: Oreo Download) 버튼을 선택하여 안
드올이드 운영체제 Image를 다운받습니다.

[그림 2-15] 안드로이드 운영체제 선택

[그림 2-16]에서 저장할 Virtual Device의 이름을 결정합니다. "Pixel XL API 27 - Wise
You"로 입력합니다.

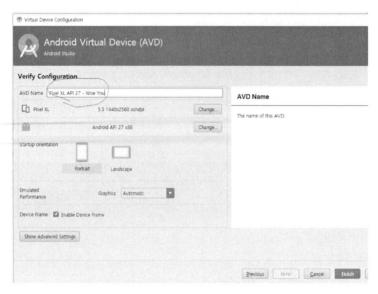

[그림 2-16] Virtual Device의 이름 결정하기

[그림 2-17]에서 생성된 Virtual Device(가짜 휴대폰)의 이름인 "Pixel XL API 27-Wise You"를 확인할 수 있습니다. 그 디바이스를 선택 후에 "OK" 버튼을 선택합니다.

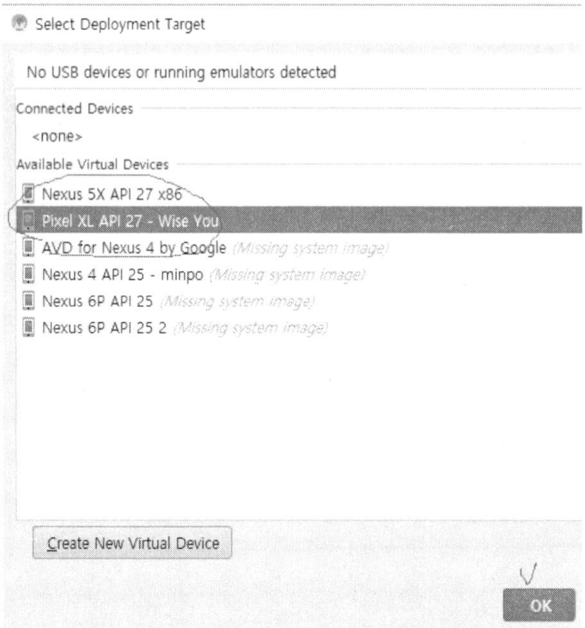

Select Deployment Target

No USB devices or running emulators detected

Connected Devices

\<none\>

Available Virtual Devices

Nexus 5X API 27 x86

Pixel XL API 27 - Wise You

AVD for Nexus 4 by Google *(Missing system image)*

Nexus 4 API 25 - minpo *(Missing system image)*

Nexus 6P API 25 *(Missing system image)*

Nexus 6P API 25 2 *(Missing system image)*

Create New Virtual Device

OK

[그림 2-17] 새롭게 생성된 Virtual Device 선택

[그림 2-18]에서 Virtual Device인 "Pixel XL API 27-Wise You"가 실행된 것을 확인할 수 있습니다. 그리고 Virtual Device에 만들어진 "Hello!! Wise You!" 앱이 실행된 것을 확인할 수 있습니다.

[그림 2-18] Virtual Device 실행 확인

"Hello!!! Wise You!"
프로그램에 자신이 다니는 대학, 학과, 학번, 이름을 출력해보자

학습목표

안드로이드 첫 프로그램을 만들 수 있다.

[그림 2-7]에서 Activity Name을 "MainActivity", Layout Name을 "activity_main"으로 지정하였습니다. Layout Name을 "activity_main.xml"으로 지정하였고, 안드로이드 화면에 나타날 여러 가지 위젯(Widget, 버튼, 그림 등)의 정보를 저장하는 파일로 정의하였습니다. Activity Name을 "MainActivity.java"으로 지정하였고 화면에 나타난 버튼 등의 다양한 위젯에 대한 행동을 정의하는 코드를 저장하는 파일로 정의하였습니다.

먼저 "activity_main.xml"와 "MainActivity.java"의 파일 위치를 Android Studio에서 찾아야 합니다. [그림 2-8]에서 "activity_main.xml"와 "MainActivity.java"의 위치를 확인할 수 있습니다. 그 파일을 마우스 더블클릭으로 열어봅니다.

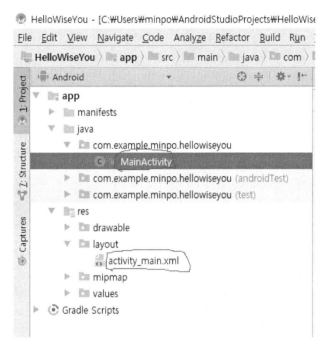

??? **[그림 2-8]** MainActivity.java, activity_main.xml 파일 열기

[그림 2-9]는 MainActivity를 더블클릭한 결과입니다. 이 파일은 안드로이드 앱을 클릭 등의 행동을 제어하기 위한 코드를 입력하는 영역입니다.

[그림 2-9] MainActivity의 내용

[그림 2-10]은 activity_main.xml을 더블클릭한 결과입니다. 이 파일은 안드로이드 앱의 화면을 설계하는 XML 파일입니다. 실행되는 앱이 화면에 나타나는 모양을 결정합니다.

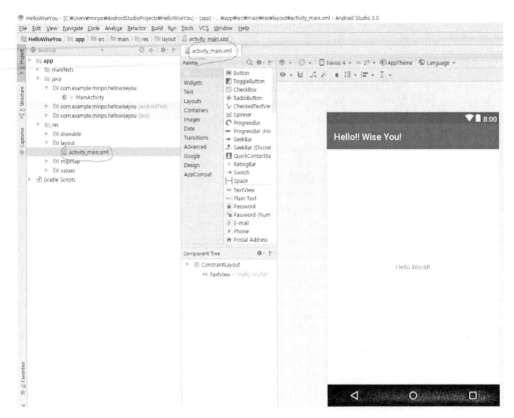

[그림 2-10] activity_main.xml의 내용

다시 프로그램 제작으로 돌아가서, 이번에는 화면에 자신이 다니는 대학, 학과, 학번, 이름을 표시하는 텍스트뷰(TextView) 위젯(Widget)을 만듭니다. [그림 2-11]은 activity_main.xml 내의 다양한 위젯을 보여주고 있습니다. 안드로이드 앱의 화면에 가져다 둘 수 있는 다양한 모양의 기능을 가지는 위젯입니다.

일반적으로 안드로이드 초급 단계의 앱 개발자는 이러한 위젯이 가지는 기능을 잘 사용할 수 있어야 합니다.

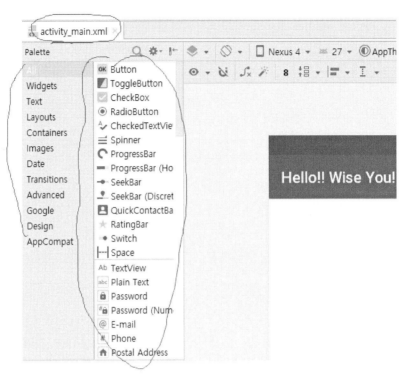

[그림 2-11] 다양한 모양의 위젯

[그림 2-12]처럼 TextView 위젯을 안드로이드 화면으로 마우스를 사용하여 옮깁니다.

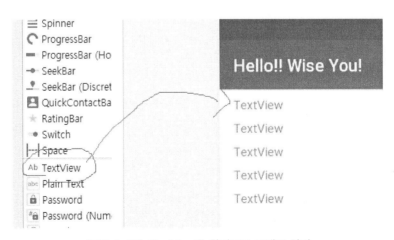

[그림 2-12] TextView를 화면으로 드래그 하기

화면으로 드래그할 때 주의할 점은 [그림 2-13]에서 TextView를 선택하면 나오는 점
(Connection) 4개가 있습니다. 각 TextView의 윗 점을 원하는 위젯에 접촉을 시켜야 화
면에 제대로 나옵니다.

[그림 2-13] Connection

TexView의 글자를 변경합니다. [그림 2-14]처럼 모든 위젯에는 해당하는 속성(Attribute)
을 가지고 있습니다. 글자를 변경하기 위해서는 속성창에서 "text"를 선택합니다. "영산대
학교"를 입력한 뒤, 반드시 엔터(Enter)키를 눌러줘야 변경됩니다.

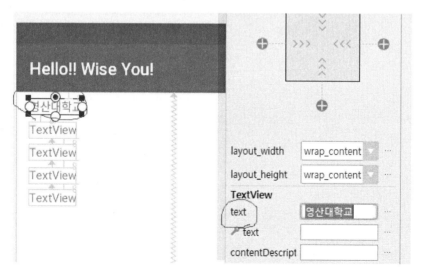

[그림 2-14] TextView의 속성창 보기

대학, 학과, 학번, 이름, 전화번호를 입력해봅니다. [그림 2-15]에서 입력한 결과를 볼 수 있습니다.

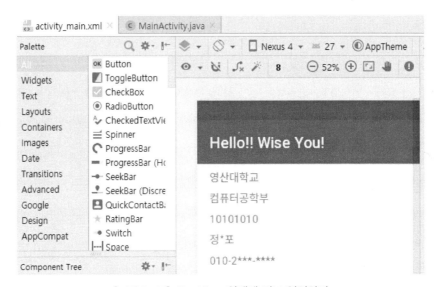

[그림 2-15] TextView 위젯에 정보 입력하기

실행 버튼(▶)을 선택하여 프로그램을 실행합니다. [그림 2-16]에서 실행결과를 확인할 수 있습니다.

[그림 2-16] 정보출력 앱 실행

참·고·자·료

[1] Kotlin 소개 자료, https://academy.realm.io/kr/posts/android-kotlin/

[2] 안드로이드 버전별 통계, https://developer.android.com/about/dashboards/index.html

Button, TextView 위젯 사용하기

이번 장에서는 Button 위젯과 TextView 위젯을 사용해 보고, 두 가지 위젯을 사용하여 응용프로그램을 만들어봅니다.

3.1 TextView 위젯 사용해보기

TextView 위젯을 사용할 수 있다.

TextView 위젯은 문자열을 화면에 표시할 때 사용하는 위젯입니다.

문자열(String)은 0개 이상의 문자들의 모임으로 정의되고 "Wise You!", "a", ""와 같이 "와 "로 둘러싸여 있습니다. 문자(Character)는 0개 또는 1개의 문자로 구성되고 'a', 'b', 'k', ''와 같이 '와 '로 둘러싸여 있습니다. TextView는 이러한 문자열을 안드로이드 디바이스의 화면에 표시하는 기능을 가진 위젯입니다.

먼저, TextView 위젯을 화면에 표시하는 과정을 살펴보겠습니다.

1) Android Studio의 Palette에서 Text를 선택하고 TextView를 선택한다.

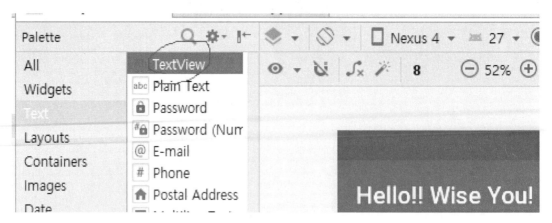

[그림 3-1] Plain Text 위젯 선택

2) 선택된 Plain Text를 Virtual Device로 Mouse Drag하여 옮긴다.

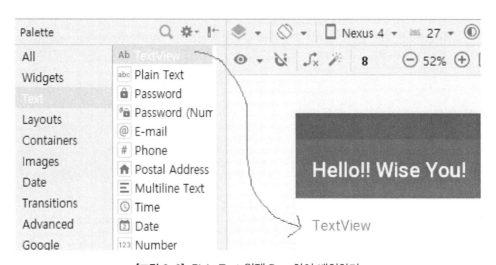

[그림 3-2] Plain Text 위젯 Drag하여 배치하기

배치를 성공하였으면, 이번에는 여러 개의 TextView를 화면에 가져다 두는 실습을 해봅니다.

[실습] 여러 개의 TextView를 화면에 가져다 두기

[그림 3-3]처럼 여러 개의 TextView 위젯을 배치시킨 뒤, 실행 시켜 보세요.
대부분의 실행 결과는 [그림 3-4]처럼 [그림 3-3]의 8개의 위젯이 하나로 보입니다.

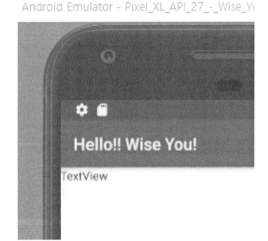

[그림 3-3] TextView 배치 화면　　　**[그림 3-4]** TextView 배치 화면 실행결과 (오류)

[그림 3-4]와 같은 배치 오류는 레이아웃(Layout)의 설정이 잘못되어 발생합니다. 먼저 레이아웃[1]은 사용자 인터페이스에 대한 시각적 구조를 정의합니다. 즉, 화면에 위젯을 배치시켜 주는 방법을 제공합니다.

Android Studio 3.0 버전은 새로운 안드로이드 앱 프로젝트를 생성하면서 "ConstraintLayout" 방식으로 위젯을 배치합니다. 여러 개의 TextView를 제대로 배치하기 위해, [그림 3-5]와 같이 상단의 "Connection"을 [그림 3-6]과 같이 상단의 타이틀 바에 밀착시킨다.

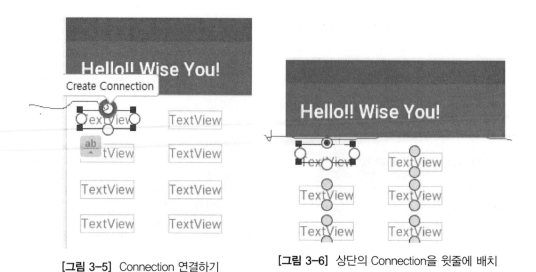

[그림 3-5] Connection 연결하기　　　　[그림 3-6] 상단의 Connection을 윗줄에 배치

이번에는 [그림 3-6]과 같이 "Connection"을 선택하고 [그림 3-7]과 같이 두 번째 TextView 의 상단 "Connection"을 첫 번째 TextView의 아래에 연결한다.

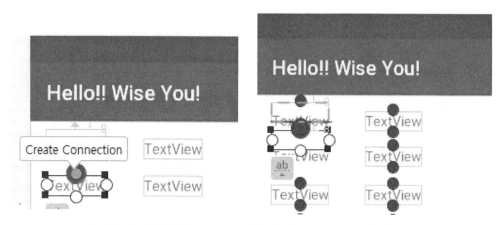

[그림 3-7] 두 번째 Connection 선택 후, 상단 TextView로 연결하기

[그림 3-8]은 배치가 완료된 화면을 보여준다.

[그림 3-8] 완성된 TextView 배치

[그림 3-8]처럼 화면의 글자에 대해 크기 변경, 색상 변경, 폰트변경 등을 하려면 TextView 속성을 익혀야 한다.

속성 이름	설명
autoLink	TextView를 링크(Link)처럼 사용할 수 있다.
breakStrategy	TextView에 표시되는 텍스트가 영역을 넘어갈 때의 정책을 결정할 수 있다.
linkclickable	TextView에 표시되는 텍스트를 클릭할 수 있게 한다.
singleLine	TextView에 표시되는 텍스트를 한 줄로 표시한다.
textColor	TextView에 표시되는 텍스트의 색상을 변경한다.
textSelectable	TextView에 표시되는 텍스트를 선택할 수 있다.
textSize	TextView에 표시되는 텍스트의 크기를 변경한다.
textStyle	TextView에 표시되는 텍스트의 스타일을 지정한다.
typeface	TextView에 표시되는 폰트를 변경한다.

[표 3-1] 자주 사용하는 TextView의 속성

3-1-1 Text를 링크(Link)로 사용하기 (autoLink)

TextView 속성 중 Text 속성에 URL이나 Email 주소가 포함되었을 때, 표시되는 텍스트를 링크 형태로 표현된다. 표시하기 위해서는, "autoLink" 속성에 설정된 값에 따라 자동으로 프로그램이 실행되고 디폴트로 설정된 프로그램으로 전달되어 실행된다.

"autoLink"에 입력되는 값은 다음과 같다.

- none : 링크 없음(기본값)
- web : 웹에서 사용되는 URL로 사용됨(웹 브라우저가 호출되어 실행됨)
- email : email로 사용됨(이메일 클라이언트가 호출되어 실행됨)
- phone : 전화번호로 사용됨(전화걸기 앱이 실행됨)
- map : 지도 주소로 사용됨(지도 앱이 실행됨)
- all : "none" 속성을 제외한 위의 모든 속성을 사용함

"autoLink" 사용시에 "web | phone"과 같이 두 가지 기능을 혼용하여 사용할 수도 있다.

android_main.xml 파일의 TextView 속성(clickable, autoLink) 예는 다음과 같다.

```
<TextView
        android:id="@+id/textView6"
        android:text="영산대는 http://www.ysu.ac.kr"
        android:clickable="true"
        android:autoLink="web" />
```

[실행결과]

Hello!! Wise You!

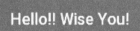
영산대는 http://www.ysu.ac.kr

(클릭하면⇒)

```
<TextView
        android:id="@+id/textView"
        android:autoLink="email"
        android:clickable="true"
        android:text="저의 email은 minpo@ysu.ac.kr입니다." />
```

[실행결과]

3-1-2 TextView의 글자가 설정된 영역을 넘어갈 때 설정하기 (breakStrategy)

TextView에 지정된 문자열이 다음 줄로 넘어갈 때, breakStragegy 속성을 사용하여 줄 넘김 정책을 결정할 수 있다. 다음의 속성 값을 설정할 수 있다.

- simple (0)
- high_quality (1)
- balanced (2)

android_main.xml 파일의 TextView 속성(breakStrategy) 예는 다음과 같다.

```
<TextView
    ~~ 생략 ~~
        android:text="이 예제는 simple 속성입니다. 이제 한 줄을 넘어갑니다.
영산대학교 abcdefghijklmnopqrstuvwxyz abcdefghijklmnopqrstuvwxyz abcdefghijklmnopqrstuvwxyz"
        android:breakStrategy="simple"
    ~~생략 ~~ />
<TextView
    ~~ 생략 ~~
        android:text="이 예제는 high_quality 속성입니다. 이제 한 줄을 넘어갑니다.
영산대학교 abcdefghijklmnopqrstuvwxyz abcdefghijklmnopqrstuvwxyz
abcdefghijklmnopqrstuvwxyz"
```

```
        android:breakStrategy="high_quality"
    ~~ 생략 ~~ />


  <TextView
    ~~ 생략 ~~
        android:text="이 예제는 balanced 속성입니다. 이제 한 줄을 넘어갑니다.
영산대학교 abcdefghijklmnopqrstuvwxyz abcdefghijklmnopqrstuvwxyz
abcdefghijklmnopqrstuvwxyz"
    ~~ 생략 ~~ />
```

[실행결과]

3-1-3 TextView에 표시되는 텍스트를 한 줄로 표시하기 (singleLine)

기본 설정 값으로 TextView에 지정된 문자열이 길어질 때 다음 줄로 넘어간다. singleLine 속성을 false 값으로 설정하면 한 줄에 출력된다. singleLine 속성은 API 레벨 3 부터는 deprecated 되었다고 한다. 대신에 maxLines 값을 사용하여 설정한다. 즉, maxLines 값을 1로 설정한다.

- 값으로 True 또는 False 값을 넣을 수 있다.
- false가 기본 값이다. 즉, 문자열이 길어지면 두 줄 이상이 만들어진다.

android_main.xml 파일의 TextView 속성(singleLine) 예는 다음과 같다.

```
<TextView
    ~~ 생략 ~~
        android:text="이 예제는 simple 속성입니다. 이제 한 줄을 넘어갑니다.
영산대학교 abcdefghijklmnopqrstuvwxyz abcdefghijklmnopqrstuvwxyz
abcdefghijklmnopqrstuvwxyz"
        android:breakStrategy="simple"
        android:singleLine="true"
    ~~생략 ~~ />
```

[실행결과]

3-1-4 TextView에 표시되는 텍스트의 컬러(Color) 변경하기 (textColor)

기본 설정 값으로 TextView에 지정된 컬러는 검정색이다. textColor 속성에 컬러 값을 설정한다. 안드로이드 컬러 값을 설정하기 위해, A(Alpha), R(Red), G(Green), B(Blue) 값을 사용한다. 각각의 값의 범위는 0에서 255까지의 값을 가진다. 일반적으로 색상은 대부분 RGB 값만을 사용한다. 컬러 값을 설정하는 방법은 #RRGGBB 형식을 사용한다. 컬러에 투명도까지 표현하고 싶다면 #AARRGGBB 형식을 사용한다.

색상을 선택할 때, 참고할 사이트는 "http://htmlcolorcodes.com/"와 "https://www.rapidtables.com/web/color/RGB_Color.html를 추천한다.

투명도 값은 RGB 컬러처럼 0에서 255까지의 값을 가질 수 있다. 투명도를 백분율로 표현할 때 계산식은 투명도백분율(1-99)×2.55로 하고 소수점은 반올림한다. 계산한 결과 값을 16진수 값으로 바꾼다. 예를 들어 투명도 10%는 10×2.55에서 계산한 26(반올림 값)을 16진수로 변경하면 1A 값이 된다. 즉, 투명도 10%인 RED 색상을 표현하고 싶다면, #1AFF0000로 설정한다. 투명도 90%인 RED 색상을 표현하고 싶다면, 90×2.55에서 계산한 230(반올림 값)을 16진수로 변경하면 E6 값이 되고, #E6FF000로 설정한다.

android_main.xml 파일의 TextView 속성(textColor) 예는 다음과 같다.

```
<TextView
    ~~ 생략 ~~
    android:textColor="#FF0000"
    android:text="이 예제는 색상 표현입니다."
    ~~생략 ~~ />
```

[실행결과]

Hello~ Y'su

이 예제는 색상 표현입니다.

```
<TextView
    ~~ 생략 ~~
    android:textColor="#E6FF0000"
    android:text="이 예제는 색상 표현입니다."
    ~~생략 ~~ />
```

[실행결과]

Hello~ Y'su

이 예제는 색상 표현입니다.

3-1-5 TextView에 표시되는 텍스트의 크기 변경하기 (textSelectable)

TextView의 textSelectable 속성은 TextView에 나타나는 글자를 선택할 수 있게 한다. 이 값의 속성은 true와 false 값을 선택할 수 있다.

android_main.xml 파일의 TextView 속성(textSelectable) 예는 다음과 같다.

```
<TextView
    ~~ 생략 ~~
        android:text="sp로 텍스트 설정, 글자 크기는 20sp 입니다."
        android:textSize="20sp"
    ~~생략 ~~ />
<TextView
    ~~ 생략 ~~
        android:text="dp로 텍스트 설정, 글자 크기는 20dp 입니다."
        android:textSize="20dp"
    ~~생략 ~~ />
```

[실행결과]

첫 번째 줄은 textSelectable 속성 값을 true로 설정하여 선택할 수 있고, 두 번째 줄은 textSelectable 속성을 false로 설정하여 선택할 수 없다.

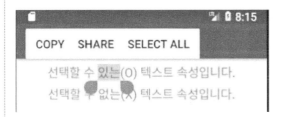

3-1-6 TextView에 표시되는 텍스트의 크기 변경하기 (textSize)

TextView의 textSize 속성은 TextView에 나타나는 글자의 크기를 변경한다. 텍스트의 크기를 표현할 때 여러 가지의 크기 단위를 사용할 수 있다. 구글에서는 sp(scaled pixel)과 dp(density-independent pixel)을 사용하도록 권장하고 있다.

안드로이드를 지원하는 디바이스는 다양한 해상도와 화면크기를 지원하기 위해 dpi는 1 인치(inch, 2.54cm)에 속하는 pixel 수를 의미한다.

안드로이드 프로그램을 개발하면서 개발된 앱이 다양한 디바이스에서 문제없이 작동되려면 해상도와 개발되는 객체(글자크기 등)와의 관계를 이해해야 한다. 이를 위해 5장의 화면 해상도 이해하기를 참고한다. 이 장에서는 간단한 예제를 제시한다.

http://angrytools.com/android/pixelcalc/ 사이트[4]를 참고하여 단위들 사이의 관계를 참고 한다.

android_main.xml 파일의 TextView 속성(textSize) 예는 다음과 같다.

```
<TextView
    ~~ 생략 ~~
    android:text="sp로 텍스트 설정, 글자 크기는 20sp 입니다."
    android:textSize="20sp"
    ~~생략 ~~ />
<TextView
    ~~ 생략 ~~
    android:text="dp로 텍스트 설정, 글자 크기는 20dp 입니다."
    android:textSize="20dp"
    ~~생략 ~~ />
```

[실행결과]

설정에서 Font 크기를 Default로 설정하면, sp와 dp는 크기가 동일한 결과로 나온다.

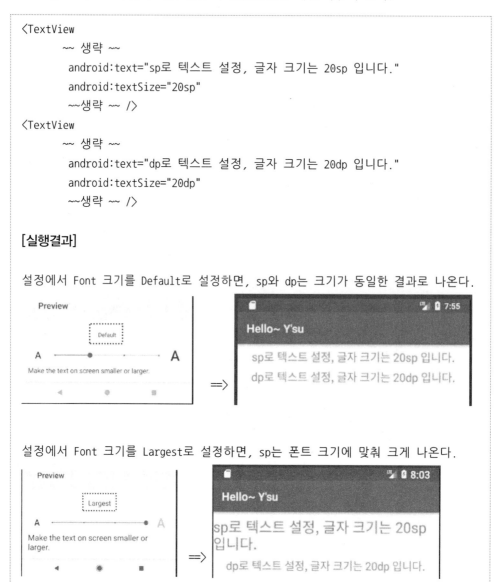

설정에서 Font 크기를 Largest로 설정하면, sp는 폰트 크기에 맞춰 크게 나온다.

설정에서 Font 크기를 Small로 설정로 설정하면, sp는 폰트 크기에 맞춰 작게 나온다.

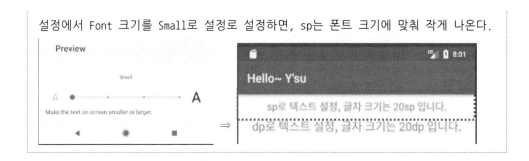

3-1-7 TextView에 표시되는 텍스트 스타일 변경하기 (textStyle)

TextView의 textStyle 속성은 TextView에 나타나는 글자의 스타일을 변경한다. 스타일에
는 "진하게", "기울이게" 속성이 있다.

- normal (0) : 기본 스타일을 의미한다. 기본 설정 값이다.

- bold (1) : 텍스트를 진하게 표시한다.

- italic (2) : 텍스트를 기울여서 표시한다.

- normal, bold, italic 속성을 하나 이상을 사용하려면 "|"를 사용한다.

예) normal | bold

android_main.xml 파일의 TextView 속성(textStyle) 예는 다음과 같다.

```
<TextView
    ~~ 생략 ~~
    android:text="텍스트-진하게 속성-입니다."
    android:textStyle="bold"
    ~~생략 ~~ />
<TextView
    ~~ 생략 ~~
    android:text=" 텍스트-진하게, 이텔릭 속성-입니다."
    android:textStyle="bold|italic"
    ~~생략 ~~ />
```

[실행결과]

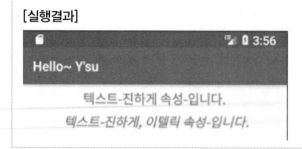

3-1-8 TextView에 표시되는 텍스트 폰트 변경하기 (typeface)

TextView의 textface 속성은 TextView에 나타나는 글자의 폰트를 변경한다. 안드로이드 디바이스에서 사용할 수 있는 폰트는 normal, sans, serif, monospace를 선택할 수 있다.

- normal (0) : 기본 폰트를 의미한다. 기본 설정 값이다.
- sans (1) : sans로 설정한다.
- serif (2) : serif로 설정한다.
- monospace (3) : monospace로 설정한다.

android_main.xml 파일의 TextView 속성(textStyle) 예는 다음과 같다.

```
<TextView
    ~~ 생략 ~~
    android:text="텍스트-normal 속성-입니다."
    android:typeface="normal"
    android:textSize="20sp"
    ~~생략 ~~ />
<TextView
    ~~ 생략 ~~
    android:text="텍스트-sans 속성-입니다."
    android:typeface="sans"
    android:textSize="20sp"
    ~~생략 ~~ />
```

```
<TextView
        ~~ 생략 ~~
        android:text="텍스트-serif 속성-입니다."
        android:typeface="serif"
        android:textSize="20sp"
        ~~생략 ~~ />
<TextView
        ~~ 생략 ~~
        android:text="텍스트-monospace 속성-입니다."
        android:typeface="monospace"
        android:textSize="20sp"
        ~~생략 ~~ />
```

[실행결과]

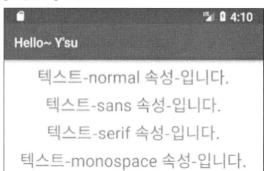

Button 위젯 사용해보기

학습목표

Button 위젯을 사용할 수 있다.

Button

```
public class Button
extends TextView
```

java.lang.Object
  ↳ android.view.View
    ↳ android.widget.TextView
      ↳ android.widget.Button

[그림 3-9] 버튼 상속도

안드로이드 Button 위젯은 화면을 터치 했을 때 발생하는 클릭 이벤트를 처리하는 기능과 텍스트와 아이콘으로 구성된다.

[그림 3-9]는 android.widget.Button의 상속 그림을 표현한다[5]. android.widget.TextView 위젯이 할 수 있는 모든 기능을 그대로 상속받는다. 즉, 부모 클래스인 TextView의 모든 기능을 Button에서 새로 만들 필요 없이 그대로 사용할 수 있다. Button은 클릭되었을 때 발생하는 이벤트 처리에 대해 추가 작업해야 한다. 버튼에 대한

이벤트 처리를 할 수 있는 방법은 두 가지 방법이 있다. 첫 번째 방법은 xml 코드에 추가하는 방법이고 두 번째 방법은 코드에 직접 추가하는 방법이다[6].

3-2-1. Button 이벤트 처리 방법 I

이 방법은 화면 처리와 관계된 Layout XML에 Button 이벤트 정보를 추가하는 방법이다. 간단한 프로그램 작성으로 사용방법을 살펴보자.

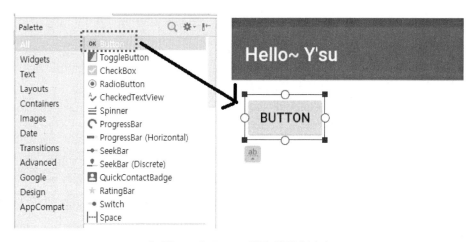

[그림 3-10] Button 위젯 화면에 넣기

[그림 3-10]처럼 Palette에서 Button 위젯을 찾은 뒤, 한 개의 버튼을 화면에 드래그하여 배치한다.

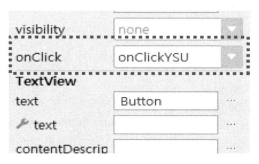

[그림 3-11] Button onClick 속성 추가

[그림 3-11]처럼 onClick 속성(Attributes)에서 onClickYSU를 입력 후, 반드시 엔터(Enter) 키를 누른다. 속성 창에 onClickYSU를 입력하고 나면 Layout을 정의하는 activity_main.xml에 자동으로 추가된다.

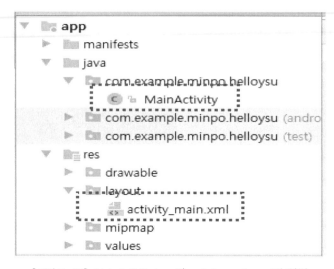

[그림 3-12] MainActivity.java와 activity_main.xml의 위치

사용될 activity_main.xml과 MainActivity.java의 위치는 [그림 3-12]와 같다. 만약 activity_main.xml과 MainActivity.java 파일이 닫혀진다면 해당 위치의 파일을 더블클릭 한다.

변경된 activity_main.xml은 다음과 같다.

```
<Button
        android:id="@+id/button"
        android:layout_width="wrap_content"
        android:layout_height="wrap_content"
        android:onClick="onClickYSU"
        android:text="Button"
        tools:layout_editor_absoluteX="16dp"
        tools:layout_editor_absoluteY="16dp" />
```

activity_main.xml 파일을 확인 후, MainActivity.java에서 Button 이벤트(event)를 추가해야 한다.

MainActivity.java에서 onCreate() 함수 내에 findViewById() 함수를 사용하여 Layout에서 추가된 Button의 정보를 얻어온다. Layout에 사용되는 모든 위젯은 위젯을 구별하기 위한 id 속성을 가진다. 현재 사용된 버튼의 id는 "button"이고 프로그램에서 사용하는 방법은 "R.id.button"으로 사용된다.

```
Button b1 = (Button) findViewById(R.id.button);
```

위의 코드를 입력하였을 때, Button 클래스에 오류가 발생된다. "Alt+Enter" 키를 눌러 위의 오류를 해결한다. 이 오류는 Button 클래스를 사용하기 위한 정보를 아래와 같이 자동 추가 된다.

```
import android.widget.Button;
```

findViewById() 함수는 Layout에 할당된 버튼 리소스를 프로그램에서 사용하기 위해 관련 정보를 얻어 온다. 완성된 코드는 다음과 같다.

```
import android.widget.Button;

public class MainActivity extends AppCompatActivity {

    @Override
    protected void onCreate(Bundle savedInstanceState) {
        super.onCreate(savedInstanceState);
        setContentView(R.layout.activity_main);

        Button b1 = (Button) findViewById(R.id.button);
    }
}
```

다음 단계는 버튼 위젯에서 발생한 특정 이벤트를 처리하기 위해 리스너(Listener)를 이용한다. 안드로이드 리스너(Listener)는 View 클래스 내에 있는 인터페이스로 하나의 콜백 메소드가 포함되어 있으며, 안드로이드에서 발생한 사건(event)을 감시하기 위한 목적으로 사용된다. 안드로이드에서 발생할 수 있는 사건(event)은 키보드, 터치 등을 의미한다. Button의 부모 클래스인 View 클래스에 포함된 Listener는 다음과 같다[6].

Listener 인터페이스	설명
onClick()	View.OnClickListener에서 온 것입니다. 사용자가 항목을 터치하거나 (터치 모드에 있을 때), 탐색 키 또는 트랙볼을 사용하여 해당 항목에 포커스를 맞추고 적절한 'Enter' 키를 누르거나 트랙볼을 누르면 호출됩니다.
onLongClick()	View.OnLongClickListener에서 온 것입니다. 사용자가 항목을 길게 누르거나(터치 모드에 있을 때), 탐색 키 또는 트랙볼을 사용하여 해당 항목에 포커스를 맞추고 적절한 'Enter' 키를 누르거나 트랙볼을 누를 때 호출됩니다(1초간).
onFocusChange()	View.OnFocusChangeListener에서 온 것입니다. 이것이 호출되는 것은 사용자가 탐색 키 또는 트랙볼을 사용하여 항목 쪽으로 이동하거나 항목에서 멀어질 때입니다.
onKey()	View.OnKeyListener에서 온 것입니다. 사용자가 항목에 포커스를 맞추고 있으면서 기기에 있는 하드웨어 키를 누르거나 키에서 손을 떼면 호출됩니다.
onTouch()	View.OnTouchListener에서 온 것입니다. 이것이 호출되는 것은 사용자가 터치 이벤트로서의 자격을 만족하는 작업을 수행하는 경우로, 여기에 누르기, 손 떼기와 화면에서 이루어지는 모든 움직임 동작(항목의 경계 내에서)이 포함됩니다.
onCreateContextMenu()	View.OnCreateContextMenuListener에서 온 것입니다. 이것을 호출하는 것은 컨텍스트 메뉴가 구축되는 중일 때입니다(정체된 "길게 클릭"의 결과로).

안드로이드 사건을 처리하기 위해, 안드로이드에서는 미리 처리하기 위한 함수를 모두 정의하고 있다.

버튼이 눌렸을 때 할 일을 정의하기 위해 다음과 같이 함수를 추가한다.

```
public void onClickYSU(View v) {
   Toast.makeText(this, "Button YSU가 눌렸습니다.", Toast.LENGTH_SHORT).show();
}
```

위의 버튼 함수의 추가로 인해, 버튼을 누를 때마다 onClickYSU() 함수가 실행되어 화면에 Button이 눌렸다는 메시지가 나오게 된다.

Toast.makeText() 함수는 화면에 Toast 형식으로 잠시 메시지를 출력하고 사라진다.

실행을 위한 전체 코드는 다음과 같다.

```
package com.example.minpo.helloysu;

import android.support.v7.app.AppCompatActivity;
import android.os.Bundle;
import android.view.View;
import android.widget.Button;
import android.widget.Toast;

public class MainActivity extends AppCompatActivity {

    @Override
    protected void onCreate(Bundle savedInstanceState) {
        super.onCreate(savedInstanceState);
        setContentView(R.layout.activity_main);

        Button b1 = (Button) findViewById(R.id.button);
    }

    public void onClickYSU(View v) {
        Toast.makeText(this, "Button YSU가 눌렸습니다.",
Toast.LENGTH_SHORT).show();
    }
}
```

[실행 결과]

3-2-2. Button 이벤트 처리 방법 II

이 방법은 첫 번째 방법처럼 화면 처리와 관계된 Layout XML에 Button 이벤트 정보를 추가하지 않고 코드에서 직접 이벤트 정보를 추가하는 방법이다.

간단한 프로그램 작성으로 사용방법을 살펴보자. [그림 3-10]처럼 버튼 한 개를 화면에 배치하자.

MainActivity.java에서 onCreate() 함수 내에 findViewById() 함수를 사용하여 Layout에서 추가된 Button의 정보를 얻어온다. Layout에 사용되는 모든 위젯은 위젯을 구별하기 위한 id 속성을 가진다. 현재 사용된 버튼의 id는 "button"이고 프로그램에서 사용하는 방법은 "R.id.button"으로 사용된다.

완성된 코드는 다음과 같다.

```
import android.widget.Button;

public class MainActivity extends AppCompatActivity {

    @Override
    protected void onCreate(Bundle savedInstanceState) {
        super.onCreate(savedInstanceState);
        setContentView(R.layout.activity_main);

        Button b1 = (Button) findViewById(R.id.button);
    }
}
```

다음 단계는 버튼 위젯에서 발생한 특정 이벤트를 처리하기 위해 리스너(Listener)를 이용한다. 버튼이 눌렸을 때 할 일을 정의하기 위해 다음과 같은 절차로 함수를 추가한다.

```
Button b1 = (Button) findViewById(R.id.button);
b1.setOnClickListener(new View.OnClickListener() {
  @Override
  public void onClick(View view) {
      Toast.makeText(MainActivity.this, "Button YSU가 눌렸습니다.",
Toast.LENGTH_SHORT).show();
    }
});
```

버튼에 대한 클릭 이벤트 발생시 호출될 onClick() 함수를 구현한 onClickListener 객체를 new 연산자를 통해 생성하고, setOnClickListener() 함수를 호출하여 Button에서 설정한다.

위의 버튼 함수의 추가로 인해, 버튼을 누를 때마다 onClick() 함수가 실행되어 화면에 Button이 눌렸다는 메시지가 나오게 된다.
Toast.makeText() 함수는 화면에 Toast 형식으로 잠시 메시지를 출력하고 사라진다.

실행을 위한 전체 코드는 다음과 같다.

```
package com.example.minpo.helloysu;

import android.support.v7.app.AppCompatActivity;
import android.os.Bundle;
import android.view.View;
import android.widget.Button;
import android.widget.Toast;

public class MainActivity extends AppCompatActivity {

    @Override
    protected void onCreate(Bundle savedInstanceState) {
        super.onCreate(savedInstanceState);
        setContentView(R.layout.activity_main);

        Button b1 = (Button) findViewById(R.id.button);
        b1.setOnClickListener(new View.OnClickListener() {
            @Override
            public void onClick(View view) {
                Toast.makeText(MainActivity.this, "Button YSU가 눌렸습니다.",
Toast.LENGTH_SHORT).show();
            }
        });
    }
}
```

3.3 응용프로그램 만들어보기

학습목표

TextView 위젯과 Button 위젯을 사용하여 응용프로그램을 만들 수 있다.

Button과 TextView를 이용하여 응용할 수 있는 예제로 다음과 같은 역할을 수행하는 프로그램을 개발한다.

조건1) 첫 번째 버튼의 이름은 '+', 두 번째 버튼의 이름은 '-'로 한다.

조건2) 첫 번째 버튼을 선택하면 값을 +1을 증가한다. 증가시킨 결과를 TextView에 표시한다.

조건3) 두 번째 버튼을 선택하면 값을 -1을 감소한다. 감소시킨 결과를 TextView에 표시한다.

조건4) 초기 값은 0으로 한다.

첫 번째 버튼, 두 번째 버튼, 결과 값을 표시하는 TextView를 화면에 배치한다.

배치된 버튼의 캡션을 '+'와 '-'로 변경하고 결과 값을 표시하는 TextView의 결과 값을 0으
로 변경한다. 각각의 버튼과 TextView를 선택해서 text 속성 값을 조건대로 변경한다.

다음 단계는 각 버튼에 대한 클릭 이벤트를 추가한다.

```java
public class MainActivity extends AppCompatActivity {

    @Override
    protected void onCreate(Bundle savedInstanceState) {
        super.onCreate(savedInstanceState);
        setContentView(R.layout.activity_main);

        Button b1 = (Button) findViewById(R.id.button);
        b1.setOnClickListener(new View.OnClickListener() {
            @Override
            public void onClick(View view) {

            }
        });
        Button b2 = (Button) findViewById(R.id.button2);
        b2.setOnClickListener(new View.OnClickListener() {
            @Override
            public void onClick(View view) {

            }
        });
    }
}
```

다음 단계는 '+' 버튼과 '-' 버튼을 선택하면 +1씩 증가, -1씩 감소시키는 것을 만들어본다. 정수 0 값을 sum이라는 변수에 초기화를 한다. sum이라는 변수에 버튼을 선택할 때마다 +1씩 증가, -1씩 감소시킨다.

```
public class MainActivity extends AppCompatActivity {
    int sum = 0;

    @Override
    protected void onCreate(Bundle savedInstanceState) {
        super.onCreate(savedInstanceState);
        setContentView(R.layout.activity_main);

        Button b1 = (Button) findViewById(R.id.button);
        b1.setOnClickListener(new View.OnClickListener() {
            @Override
            public void onClick(View view) {
                sum = sum + 1;
            }
        });
        Button b2 = (Button) findViewById(R.id.button2);
        b2.setOnClickListener(new View.OnClickListener() {
            @Override
            public void onClick(View view) {
                sum = sum - 1;
            }
        });
    }
}
```

다음 단계는 sum 값을 TextView에 표시한다.

sum 값은 정수(Integer)만 저장할 수 있는 저장소(변수)이다. Integer.toString()은 정수를 문자열로 변경하는 기능을 가진 함수이다. TextView에 표시되는 문장은 모두 문자열이기 때문에 Integer.toString(sum) 함수를 통해 TextView에 표시될 수 있는 문자열로 변경해야 한다.

```java
public class MainActivity extends AppCompatActivity {
    int sum = 0;

    @Override
    protected void onCreate(Bundle savedInstanceState) {
        super.onCreate(savedInstanceState);
        setContentView(R.layout.activity_main);

        final TextView tv = (TextView) findViewById(R.id.textView6);

        Button b1 = (Button) findViewById(R.id.button);
        b1.setOnClickListener(new View.OnClickListener() {
            @Override
            public void onClick(View view) {
                sum = sum + 1;
                tv.setText(Integer.toString(sum));
            }
        });
        Button b2 = (Button) findViewById(R.id.button2);
        b2.setOnClickListener(new View.OnClickListener() {
            @Override
            public void onClick(View view) {
                sum = sum - 1;
                tv.setText(Integer.toString(sum));
            }
        });
    }
}
```

[실행결과]

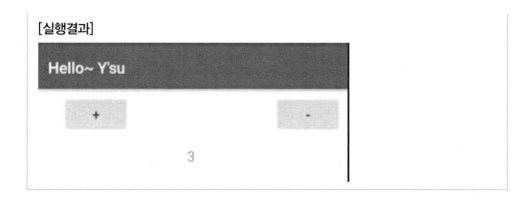

참·고·자·료

[1] 안드로이드 레이아웃(Layout)의 정의,
"https://developer.android.com/guide/topics/ ui/declaring-layout.htm"

[2] 안드로이드 TextView 속성 정의,
"https://developer.android.com/reference/ android/widget/TextView.html"

[3] 색상 선택 사이트, "https://www.rapidtables.com/web/color/RGB_Color.html",
"http://htmlcolorcodes.com/"

[4] 안드로이드 단위(sp, dp) 참고 사이트, http://angrytools.com/android/pixelcalc/

[5] Button 위젯 상속도, https://developer.android.com/reference/android/widget/
Button.html

[6] 안드로이드 입력 이벤트 참고 사이트,
https://developer.android.com/guide/topics/ui/ui-events.html,
https://developer.android.com/guide/topics/ui/controls/button.html?hl=ko

EditText 위젯 사용해보기

이번 장에서는 EditText 위젯을 사용해 보고, 지금까지 배운 위젯으로 응용프로그램을 만들어봅니다.

4.1 EditText 위젯 사용해보기

EditText 위젯을 사용할 수 있다.

EditText 위젯은 키보드 입력을 사용하여 임의의 정보를 입력할 때 그 입력을 처리해주는 위젯이다.

EditText

```
public class EditText
extends TextView
```

java.lang.Object
  ㄴ android.view.View
      ㄴ android.widget.TextView
          ㄴ android.widget.EditText

[그림 4-1] 버튼 상속도

[그림 4-1]은 EditText의 상속도를 보여준다[1]. EditText의 부모 클래스는 TextView이다. TextView의 텍스트를 출력하는 기능을 기본적으로 제공하고 EditText는 추가로 입력 기능까지 제공한다.

먼저 EditText를 간단히 사용해보자.

[그림 4-2] Plain Text (EditText) 선택   ⇒   **[그림 4-3]** 화면에 드래그하여 배치하기

[그림 4-2]에서 EditText 위젯의 대표인 Plain Text를 선택하여 [그림 4-3]처럼 드래그 (drag)하여 배치한다. 앱이 처음 실행될 때, EditText의 첫 글자를 "Y'su Fighting. This is Edit Text"로 표시해보자.

[그림 4-4]처럼 text 속성(attribute)에 "Y'su Fighting. This is Edit Text"를 입력 후 'Enter' 키를 입력한다. [그림 4-5]는 실행 결과이다.

```
〈EditText
    android:id="@+id/editText2"
    android:layout_width="wrap_content"
    android:layout_height="wrap_content"
    android:layout_marginEnd="8dp"
    android:layout_marginStart="8dp"
    android:layout_marginTop="8dp"
    android:ems="10"
    android:inputType="textPersonName"
    android:text="Y'su Fighting. This is Edit Text"
    app:layout_constraintEnd_toEndOf="parent"
    app:layout_constraintStart_toStartOf="parent"
    app:layout_constraintTop_toTopOf="parent"
/〉
```

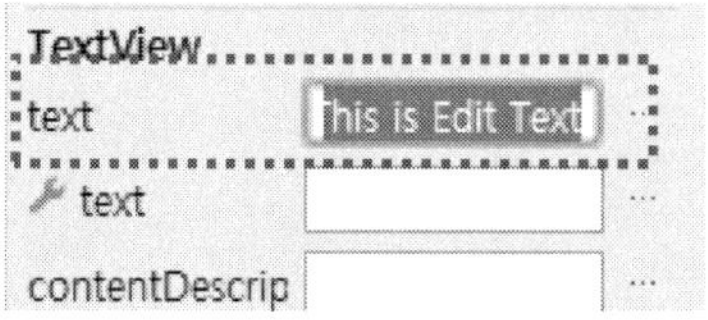

[그림 4-4] text 속성 변경

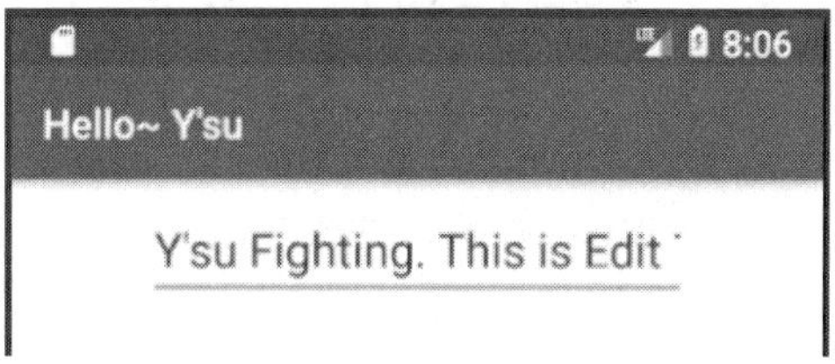

[그림 4-5] 실행 결과

4.2 EditText 위젯의 Text를 변경하기

[그림 4-4]에서처럼 android:text 속성을 통해 변경할 수 있다. 또 다른 방법으로 JAVA code에서도 변경할 수 있다.

4-1절에서 EditText의 id는 "editText2"로 설정되어 있다. findViewById() 함수를 통해 Layout 리소스에 저장된 정보를 읽어올 수 있다.
findViewById()에 의해 얻은 참조 변수 et를 사용하여 setText()함수를 사용하여 텍스트를 수정할 수 있다. setText()함수는 android:text와 같은 의미이다.

```java
public class MainActivity extends AppCompatActivity {
    int sum = 0;

    @Override
    protected void onCreate(Bundle savedInstanceState) {
        super.onCreate(savedInstanceState);
        setContentView(R.layout.activity_main);

        EditText et = (EditText) findViewById(R.id.editText2);
        et.setText("영산대학교 컴퓨터공학부");
    }
```

[실행 결과]

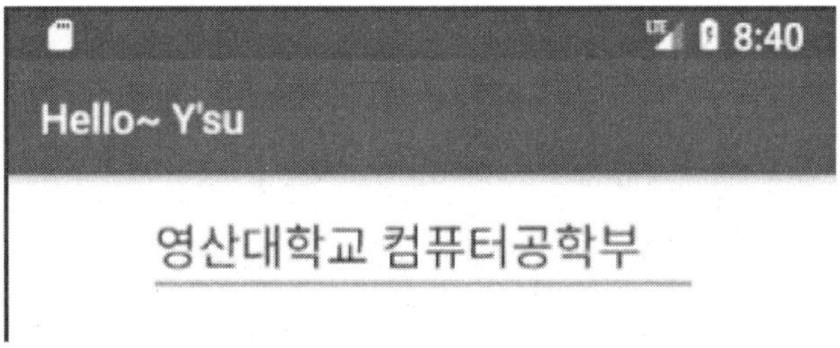

Hello~ Y'su

영산대학교 컴퓨터공학부

EditText의 내용을 읽은 뒤, 수정하기

EditText를 사용하기 위해 반드시 익혀야 하는 기능은 입력된 텍스트를 읽어 들이고 그 내용을 수정할 수 있는 기능이다. 이 기능을 사용하기 위해, 두 개의 EditText를 만들고, 첫 번째 EditText에서 읽어 들인 내용을 두 번째 EditText에 입력하는 기능을 프로그램 한다. 먼저 EditText 내용을 프로그램에서 아무것도 없는 "" 문자열로 설정하기 위해 setText("") 함수를 사용한다.

```
EditText et1 = (EditText) findViewById(R.id.editText2);
et1.setText("");
EditText et2 = (EditText) findViewById(R.id.editText3);
et2.setText("");
```

이번에는 첫 번째 EditText에서 입력된 결과를 읽어들인 결과를 두 번째 EditText에 설정을 해보자. 입력된 결과를 읽을 때 getText() 함수를 사용한다. getText() 함수의 경우에는 Editable 인터페이스 타입을 리턴한다. Editable 인터페이스로 리턴된 값은 스트링(String) 값으로 변환해야만 setText(String) 함수에서 사용할 수 있다. toString() 함수를 사용하여 변환한다.

```
EditText et1 = (EditText) findViewById(R.id.editText2);
et1.setText("영산대학교");

EditText et2 = (EditText) findViewById(R.id.editText3);

String firstText = et1.getText().toString();
et2.setText(firstText);
```

EditText의 입력 변화 이벤트 받기
(addTextChangedListener)

addTextChangedListener는 EditText에 사용자가 텍스트를 입력할 때 유용하게 사용된다. 입력되는 텍스트가 바뀔 때마다 리스너 이벤트가 작동된다.
addTextChangedListener는 세 가지 함수를 기본적으로 사용한다.

- beforeTextChanged(CharSequence charSequence, int i, int i1, int i2)

　i(start) 지점에서 시작되는 i1(before) 개수만큼의 글자들이 i2(count) 개수만큼의 글자들로 대치되었을 때 호출된다.

- onTextChanged(CharSequence charSequence, int i, int i1, int i2)

　i(start) 지점에서 시작되는 i1(count) 개수만큼의 글자들이 i2(after) 길이만큼의 글자로 대치되려고 할 때 호출된다.

- afterTextChanged(Editable editable)

　EditText의 텍스트가 변경되면 호출된다.

```
EditText et1 = (EditText) findViewById(R.id.editText2);
et1.setText("");

et1.addTextChangedListener(new TextWatcher() {
@Override
    public void beforeTextChanged(CharSequence charSequence, int i, int i1, int
i2) {
            //입력 전
    }
```

```
    @Override
    public void onTextChanged(CharSequence charSequence, int i, int i1, int i2)
{
            //입력되는 텍스트가 변경될 때
    }

    @Override
    public void afterTextChanged(Editable editable) {
        // 입력하기 전
    }
});
```

4.5 응용프로그램 만들어보기 I

학습목표

지금까지 배운 EditText, Button, TextView를 사용하여, 사용하면 안되는 단어를 체크하는 프로그램을 만들어보자.

먼저, setHint() 함수를 사용하여 사용자에게 안내 멘트를 EditText에 출력하자.

```
EditText et1 = (EditText) findViewById(R.id.editText2);
et1.setText("");
et1.setHint("단어를 입력하세요!");
```

[실행 결과]

Hello~ Y'su

단어를 입력하세요!

4-4절에서 설명한 addTextChangedListener 코드를 추가한다.

```
EditText et1 = (EditText) findViewById(R.id.editText2);
et1.setText("");
et1.setHint("단어를 입력하세요!");

et1.addTextChangedListener(new TextWatcher() {
```

```
    @Override
    public void beforeTextChanged(CharSequence charSequence, int i, int i1, int
i2) {
        //입력 전
    }
    @Override
    public void onTextChanged(CharSequence charSequence, int i, int i1, int i2)
{
        //입력되는 텍스트가 변경될 때
    }
    @Override
    public void afterTextChanged(Editable editable) {
        // 입력 후
    }
});
```

금칙어가 나오면 경고가 표시될 TextView를 만든다.

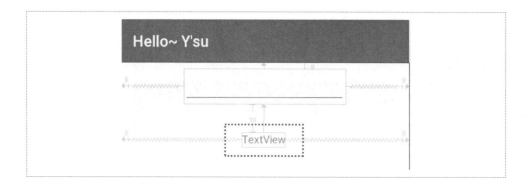

금지어로 사용될 단어를 정의한다. JAVA 언어의 배열[2]을 사용한다.

```
String []stopWord = {
            "dislike",
            "bad",
            "xxx"
    };
```

금지어가 결정되었으면, 입력할 때마다 금지어인지 아닌지 검사(Check)를 한다. 금지어일 경우에 "경고 : 단어"가 나오고 금지아가 아닐 경우에는 "좋은 단어"라고 출력되게 한다.

```java
public void afterTextChanged(Editable editable) {
    int i;
    for(i=0;i<stopWord.length;i++) {
        if (editable.toString().equals(stopWord[i])) {
            tv.setTextColor(Color.RED);
            tv.setText("경고 : " + stopWord[i]);
        }
        else {
            tv.setTextColor(Color.BLACK);
            tv.setText("좋은 단어");
        }
    }
}
```

이제 완성된 코드를 살펴보자.

```java
public class MainActivity extends AppCompatActivity {
    String []stopWord = {
            "dislike",
            "bad",
            "xxx"
    };
    @Override
    protected void onCreate(Bundle savedInstanceState) {
        super.onCreate(savedInstanceState);
        setContentView(R.layout.activity_main);

        EditText et1 = (EditText) findViewById(R.id.editText2);
        et1.setText("");
        et1.setHint("단어를 입력하세요!");
```

```java
        final TextView tv = (TextView) findViewById(R.id.textView7);
        tv.setTextSize(20);
        tv.setTextColor(Color.RED);
        tv.setText("");

        et1.addTextChangedListener(new TextWatcher() {
            @Override
            public void beforeTextChanged(CharSequence charSequence, int i,
int i1, int i2) {
                //입력 전
            }

            @Override
            public void onTextChanged(CharSequence charSequence, int i, int
i1, int i2) {
                //입력되는 텍스트가 변경될 때
            }

            @Override
            public void afterTextChanged(Editable editable) {
                // 입력후
                int i;
                for(i=0;i<stopWord.length;i++) {
                    if (editable.toString().equals(stopWord[i])) {
                        tv.setTextColor(Color.RED);
                        tv.setText("경고 : " + stopWord[i]);
                    }
                    else {
                        tv.setTextColor(Color.BLACK);
                        tv.setText("좋은 단어");
                    }
                }
            }
        });

    }
}
```

[실행 결과]

⇒ 첫 화면

⇒ 금지어가 아닌 문자열 입력

⇒ 금지어 입력

4.6 응용프로그램 만들어보기 II

학습목표

지금까지 배운 EditText, Button, TextView를 사용하여, 특정 단어("전화", "네이버", "영산대 컴퓨터 공학부"가 입력되면 해당 화면으로 가는 프로그램을 만들어보자.

아래의 화면처럼 EditText 1개와 TextView 1개를 배치하자.

TextView에 나타나는 단어는 "phone", "naver", "ysucomputer"를 사용한다. phone은 전화번호를 실행하는 화면을 실행한다. "naver"는 웹브라워저를 실해하여 m.naver.com에 접속하는 화면을 실행한다. "ysucomuter"는 영산대학교 컴퓨터공학부 홈페이지(ce.ysu.ac.kr)에 접속하는 화면을 실행한다.

> ### Hello~ Y'su
>
> _____
>
> 사용 가능 단어 : phone, naver, ysucomputer

안드로이드 앱은 네 가지 기본 구성요소 "Activity", "Service", "Broadcast Receiver", "Content Provider"가 있다. 구체적인 사항은 본 교재의 2권에서 살펴보도록 한다. 이 예제에서는 네 가지 구성요소 간의 정보를 전달할 수 있는 인텐트(Intent)를 사용한다. 안드로이드 내의 기본 앱인 전화, 카메라, 연락처, 문자 등을 인텐트를 이용하여 호출한다.

인텐트를 호출하기 위해서는 AndroidManifest.xml에서 사용자 권한인 permission 설정을 해야 한다.

전화를 걸거나 전화 다이얼 번호를 표시해주는 화면을 이용하기 위해서는 다음과 같은 퍼미션을 사용한다.

```
Android ▼ ⊕ ÷ | ⚙▾ ǀ←
▼ app
    ▼ manifests
        AndroidManifest.xml
    ▼ java
```

```xml
<?xml version="1.0" encoding="utf-8"?>
<manifest xmlns:android="http://schemas.android.com/apk/res/android"
    package="com.example.minpo.helloysu">

    <uses-permission android:name="android.permission.CALL_PHONE" />

    <application
        android:allowBackup="true"
        android:icon="@mipmap/ic_launcher"
        android:label="@string/app_name"
        android:roundIcon="@mipmap/ic_launcher_round"
        android:supportsRtl="true"
        android:theme="@style/AppTheme">
        <activity android:name=".MainActivity">
            <intent-filter>
                <action android:name="android.intent.action.MAIN" />

                <category android:name="android.intent.category.LAUNCHER" />
            </intent-filter>
        </activity>
    </application>

</manifest>
```

Intent를 사용하여 전화번호를 실행할 수 있는 코드는 다음과 같다. 전화번호를 같이 실행하기 위해서는 Intent in = new Intent(Intent.ACTION_VIEW, Uri.parse("tel:"));에서 Intent in = new Intent(Intent.ACTION_VIEW, Uri.parse("tel:123-4568-1234"));를 입력한다.

```java
public class MainActivity extends AppCompatActivity {
    @Override
    protected void onCreate(Bundle savedInstanceState) {
        super.onCreate(savedInstanceState);
        setContentView(R.layout.activity_main);

        EditText et1 = (EditText) findViewById(R.id.editText2);
        et1.setText("");
        et1.setHint("하고자하는 명령입력 바람!");

        et1.addTextChangedListener(new TextWatcher() {
            @Override
            public void beforeTextChanged(CharSequence charSequence, int i,
int i1, int i2) {
                //입력 전
            }
            @Override
            public void onTextChanged(CharSequence charSequence, int i, int
i1, int i2) {
                //입력되는 텍스트가 변경될 때
            }
            @Override
            public void afterTextChanged(Editable editable) {
                // 입력후
                if(editable.toString().equals("phone")) {
                    Intent in = new Intent(Intent.ACTION_VIEW, Uri.parse("tel:"));
                    startActivity(in);
                    editable.clear();

                } else if(editable.toString().equals("naver")) {


                } else if(editable.toString().equals("ysucomputer")) {
```

```
                }
            }
        });
    }
}
```

naver 사이트와 영산대 컴퓨터공학부 모바일 브라우저로 접속하기 위해 다음과 같은 코
드를 입력한다.

```
public class MainActivity extends AppCompatActivity {
    @Override
    protected void onCreate(Bundle savedInstanceState) {
        super.onCreate(savedInstanceState);
        setContentView(R.layout.activity_main);

        EditText et1 = (EditText) findViewById(R.id.editText2);
        et1.setText("");
        et1.setHint("하고자하는 명령입력 바람!");

        et1.addTextChangedListener(new TextWatcher() {
            @Override
            public void beforeTextChanged(CharSequence charSequence, int i,
            int i1, int i2) {
                //입력 전
            }
            @Override
            public void onTextChanged(CharSequence charSequence, int i, int
            i1, int i2) {
                //입력되는 텍스트가 변경될 때
            }
            @Override
            public void afterTextChanged(Editable editable) {
                // 입력후
                if(editable.toString().equals("phone")) {
                    Intent    in    =    new    Intent(Intent.ACTION_VIEW,
                    Uri.parse("tel:"));
```

```
            startActivity(in);
            editable.clear();

        } else if(editable.toString().equals("naver")) {
            Intent in = new Intent(Intent.ACTION_VIEW,
                        Uri.parse("http://m.naver.com"));
            startActivity(in);
            editable.clear();
        } else if(editable.toString().equals("ysucomputer")) {
            Intent in = new Intent(Intent.ACTION_VIEW,
                        Uri.parse("http://ce.ysu.ac.kr"));
            startActivity(in);
            editable.clear();
        }
    }
});
    }
}
```

[실행 결과]

- phone 입력

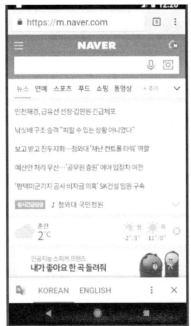

- naver 입력

- ysucomputer 입력

다음 코드는 다양한 인텐트 호출 예제이다.

```
// 임의의 웹페이지 실행하기
Uri uri = Uri.parse("http://www.google.com");
Intent in  = new Intent(Intent.ACTION_VIEW, uri);
startActivity(in);

//영산대학교 위도, 경도:35.4287887,129.14594999999997
// 구글지도 실행하기
Uri uri = Uri.parse("geo:35.4287887,129.14594999999997");
Intent it = new Intent(Intent.ACTION_VIEW,uri);
startActivity(it);

// 전화 걸기 실행하기
Uri uri = Uri.parse("tel:123-1234-1234");
Intent in = new Intent(Intent.ACTION_DIAL, uri);
startActivity(in);

// SMS/MMS 발송
Intent in = new Intent(Intent.ACTION_SENDTO, Uri.parse("smsto:" +
             "01028050969"));
in.putExtra("sms_body", "message 보냅니다.");
startActivity(in);

<uses-permission android:name="android.permission.RECEIVE_SMS" />
<uses-permission android:name="android.permission.INTERNET" />
<uses-permission android:name="android.permission.RECEIVE_MMS" />
<uses-permission android:name="android.permission.READ_SMS" />
<uses-permission android:name="android.permission.RECEIVE_WAP_PUSH" />
<uses-permission android:name="android.permission.WRITE_SMS" />
<uses-permission android:name="android.permission.SEND_SMS" />

// MMS 발송
Uri uri = Uri.parse("content://media/external/images/media/23");
Intent in = new Intent(Intent.ACTION_SEND);
in.putExtra("sms_body", "some text");
in.putExtra(Intent.EXTRA_STREAM, uri);
in.setType("image/png");
```

```
startActivity(in);

// 이메일 발송
Uri uri = Uri.parse("mailto:minpo@ysu.ac.kr");
Intent in = new Intent(Intent.ACTION_SENDTO, uri);
startActivity(in);

// 이메일 발송
Intent in = new Intent(Intent.ACTION_SEND);
in.putExtra(Intent.EXTRA_EMAIL, "minpo@ysu.ac.kr");
in.putExtra(Intent.EXTRA_TEXT, "The email body text!! Good Morning");
in.setType("text/plain");
startActivity(Intent.createChooser(in, "Choose Email Client"));

// 이메일 발송
Intent in = new Intent(Intent.ACTION_SEND);
String[] tos = {"minpo@ysu.ac.kr"};
String[] ccs = {"minpo@naver.com"};
in.putExtra(Intent.EXTRA_EMAIL, tos);
in.putExtra(Intent.EXTRA_CC, ccs);
in.putExtra(Intent.EXTRA_TEXT, "The email body text");
in.putExtra(Intent.EXTRA_SUBJECT, "The email subject text");
in.setType("message/rfc822");
startActivity(Intent.createChooser(in, "Choose Email Client"));

// extra 추가하기
Intent in = new Intent(Intent.ACTION_SEND);
in.putExtra(Intent.EXTRA_SUBJECT, "The email subject text");
in.putExtra(Intent.EXTRA_STREAM, "file:///sdcard/song.mp3");
in.setType("audio/mp3");
startActivity(Intent.createChooser(in, "Choose Email Client"));

// 구글 검색
Intent in = new Intent();
in.setAction(Intent.ACTION_WEB_SEARCH);
in.putExtra(SearchManager.QUERY,"영산대학교 컴퓨터공학부를 찾아라");
startActivity(in);
```

응용프로그램 만들어보기 III

4.7

학습목표

지금까지 배운 EditText, Button, TextView를 사용하여, 계산기 프로그램 만들어보자.

첫 번째 수와 두 번째 수를 입력 받기 위한 EditText 2개, 사칙 연산을 연산하기 위한 4개의 버튼, 결산 결과를 바로 보여주는 TextView 1개를 아래의 [그림 4-6]처럼 디자인한다.

Hello~ Y'su

| + | - |
| * | / |

결과값

[그림 4-6] 계산기 실행 화면 디자인

프로그램의 조건은 다음과 같다.

1) +, -, *, / 버튼을 선택하면, 선택된 연산으로 계속 계산한다.

2) 선택된 버튼은 background color를 YELLOW로 설정한다.

3) 0으로 나누어지거나 숫자가 아닌 정보가 들어오면 오류 메시지를 결과 값에 출력한다.

구현된 코드는 아래와 같다.

```java
public class MainActivity extends AppCompatActivity {
    float first = 0f;
    float second = 0f;
    float result = 0f;
    int defaultStatus = 0; //0 : plus, 1:minus, 2: multiply, 3: divide

    @Override
    protected void onCreate(Bundle savedInstanceState) {
        super.onCreate(savedInstanceState);
        setContentView(R.layout.activity_main);

        final EditText et1 = (EditText) findViewById(R.id.editText5);
        et1.setText("");
        et1.setHint("첫 번째 수를 입력하세요.");

        final EditText et2 = (EditText) findViewById(R.id.editText6);
        et2.setText("");
        et2.setHint("두 번째 수를 입력하세요.");

        final TextView tv = (TextView) findViewById(R.id.textView10);
        tv.setText("");
        tv.setTextSize(20);
        tv.setTextColor(Color.RED);

        final Button plus = (Button) findViewById(R.id.button3);
        plus.setBackgroundColor(Color.YELLOW);
        defaultStatus = 0; //plus
        final Button minus = (Button) findViewById(R.id.button4);
        final Button multiiply = (Button) findViewById(R.id.button5);
        final Button devide = (Button) findViewById(R.id.button6);
```

```
plus.setOnClickListener(new View.OnClickListener() {
        @Override
        public void onClick(View view) {
            defaultStatus = 0;
            plus.setBackgroundColor(Color.YELLOW);
            minus.setBackgroundColor(Color.WHITE);
            multiiply.setBackgroundColor(Color.WHITE);
            devide.setBackgroundColor(Color.WHITE);
            try {
                first = Float.parseFloat(et1.getText().toString());
                second = Float.parseFloat(et2.getText().toString());

                if(defaultStatus == 0) {
                    tv.setText((first + second) + "");
                } else if(defaultStatus == 1) {
                    tv.setText((first - second) + "");
                } else if(defaultStatus == 2) {
                    tv.setText((first * second) + "");
                } else {
                    tv.setText((first / second) + "");
                }
            } catch (NumberFormatException nfe) {
                tv.setText("수식이 완성되지 안았습니다.");
            }
        }
    });
    minus.setOnClickListener(new View.OnClickListener() {
        @Override
        public void onClick(View view) {
            defaultStatus = 1;
            plus.setBackgroundColor(Color.WHITE);
            minus.setBackgroundColor(Color.YELLOW);
            multiiply.setBackgroundColor(Color.WHITE);
            devide.setBackgroundColor(Color.WHITE);
            try {
                first = Float.parseFloat(et1.getText().toString());
                second = Float.parseFloat(et2.getText().toString());
```

```
                    if(defaultStatus == 0) {
                        tv.setText((first + second) + "");
                    } else if(defaultStatus == 1) {
                        tv.setText((first - second) + "");
                    } else if(defaultStatus == 2) {
                        tv.setText((first * second) + "");
                    } else {
                        tv.setText((first / second) + "");
                    }
                } catch (NumberFormatException nfe) {
                    tv.setText("수식이 완성되지 안았습니다.");
                }
            }
        });
        multiiply.setOnClickListener(new View.OnClickListener() {
            @Override
            public void onClick(View view) {
                defaultStatus = 2;
                plus.setBackgroundColor(Color.WHITE);
                minus.setBackgroundColor(Color.WHITE);
                multiiply.setBackgroundColor(Color.YELLOW);
                devide.setBackgroundColor(Color.WHITE);
                try {
                    first = Float.parseFloat(et1.getText().toString());
                    second = Float.parseFloat(et2.getText().toString());

                    if(defaultStatus == 0) {
                        tv.setText((first + second) + "");
                    } else if(defaultStatus == 1) {
                        tv.setText((first - second) + "");
                    } else if(defaultStatus == 2) {
                        tv.setText((first * second) + "");
                    } else {
                        tv.setText((first / second) + "");
                    }
                } catch (NumberFormatException nfe) {
                    tv.setText("수식이 완성되지 안았습니다.");
                }
            }
        });
```

```
        devide.setOnClickListener(new View.OnClickListener() {
            @Override
            public void onClick(View view) {
                defaultStatus = 3;
                plus.setBackgroundColor(Color.WHITE);
                minus.setBackgroundColor(Color.WHITE);
                multiiply.setBackgroundColor(Color.WHITE);
                devide.setBackgroundColor(Color.YELLOW);
                try {
                    first = Float.parseFloat(et1.getText().toString());
                    second = Float.parseFloat(et2.getText().toString());

                    if(defaultStatus == 0) {
                        tv.setText((first + second) + "");
                    } else if(defaultStatus == 1) {
                        tv.setText((first - second) + "");
                    } else if(defaultStatus == 2) {
                        tv.setText((first * second) + "");
                    } else {
                        tv.setText((first / second) + "");
                    }
                } catch (NumberFormatException nfe) {
                    tv.setText("수식이 완성되지 안았습니다.");
                }
            }
        });


        et1.addTextChangedListener(new TextWatcher() {
            @Override
            public void beforeTextChanged(CharSequence charSequence, int i,
int i1, int i2) {
                //입력 전
            }
            @Override
            public void onTextChanged(CharSequence charSequence, int i, int
i1, int i2) {
                //입력되는 텍스트가 변경될 때
            }
```

```java
        @Override
        public void afterTextChanged(Editable editable) {
            // 입력후

            try {
                first = Float.parseFloat(editable.toString());
                second = Float.parseFloat(et2.getText().toString());

                if(defaultStatus == 0) {
                    tv.setText((first + second) + "");
                } else if(defaultStatus == 1) {
                    tv.setText((first - second) + "");
                } else if(defaultStatus == 2) {
                    tv.setText((first * second) + "");
                } else {
                    tv.setText((first / second) + "");
                }
            } catch (NumberFormatException nfe) {
                tv.setText("수식이 완성되지 않았습니다.");
            }

        }
    });


    et2.addTextChangedListener(new TextWatcher() {
        @Override
        public void beforeTextChanged(CharSequence charSequence, int i,
int i1, int i2) {
            //입력 전
        }

        @Override
        public void onTextChanged(CharSequence charSequence, int i, int
i1, int i2) {
            //입력되는 텍스트가 변경될 때
        }
```

```
                @Override
                public void afterTextChanged(Editable editable) {
                    // 입력후
                    try {
                        first = Float.parseFloat(et1.getText().toString());
                        second = Float.parseFloat(editable.toString());

                        if(defaultStatus == 0) {
                            tv.setText((first + second) + "");
                        } else if(defaultStatus == 1) {
                            tv.setText((first - second) + "");
                        } else if(defaultStatus == 2) {
                            tv.setText((first * second) + "");
                        } else {
                            tv.setText((first / second) + "");
                        }
                    } catch (NumberFormatException nfe) {
                        tv.setText("수식이 완성되지 않았습니다.");
                    }
                }
            });

        }
    }
```

[실행 결과]

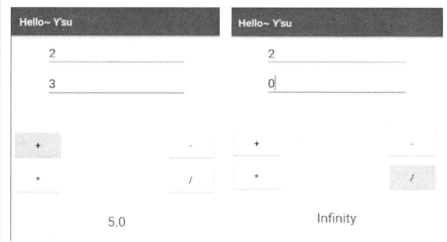

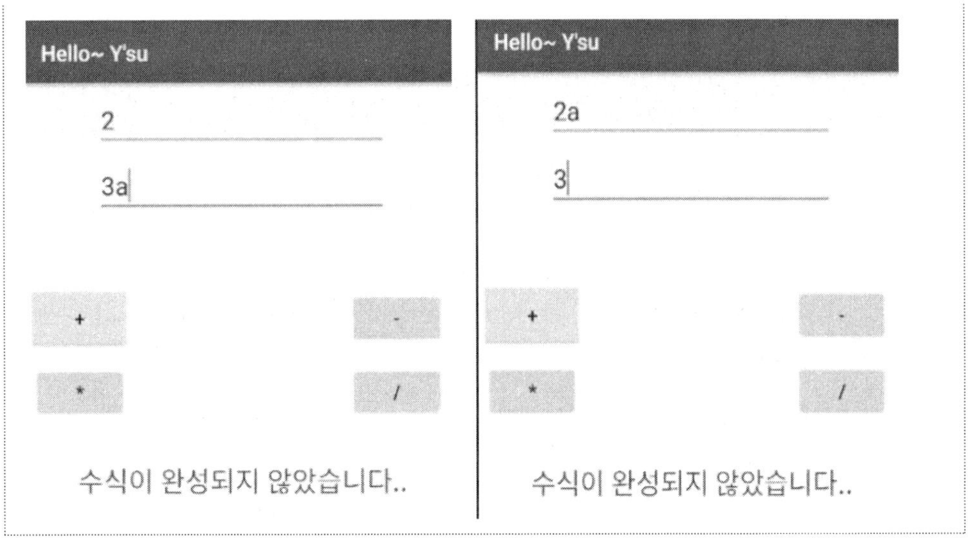

Hello~ Y'su

2

3a|

| + | | - |
| * | | / |

수식이 완성되지 않았습니다..

Hello~ Y'su

2a

3|

| + | | - |
| * | | / |

수식이 완성되지 않았습니다..

참·고·자·료

[1] Button 위젯 상속도, https://developer.android.com/reference/android/widget/
EditText.html

[2] JAVA 배열(Array), https://docs.oracle.com/javase/tutorial/java/nutsandbolts/
arrays.html

05

화면 해상도 이해하기

이번 장에서는 화면 해상도와 dpi, px, dp, dip, sp의 개념을 이해하고 실습한다.

5.1 dpi, px, dp, dip, sp의 이해

학습목표

dpi, px, dp, dip, sp를 이해한다.

dpi는 Dot Per Inch의 약어이다. 1 인치(inch)에 포함된 픽셀(pixel) 수를 의미한다. 1 인치는 2.54cm이다.

dp 또는 dip는 Density Independent Pixels의 약어이다. 크기가 다른 dpi의 단말기에서도 1 dp는 동일한 크기를 의미한다. dp는 160dpi(mdpi)를 기준으로 어떤 dpi에서도 동일한 크기와 위치를 표현할 수 있다. 기준은 mdpi이고 1dp가 1px이다. 예를 들어, mdpi를 기준으로 하여 100px 높이가 설정되었다면 100dp를 사용하면 된다.

mdpi는 구형 단말기에서 사용하기 때문에 요즘은 xhdpi를 많이 사용한다. xhdpi는 mdpi의 2배밀도이기 때문에 10px는 5dp로 사용된다. 아래의 표에서 dpi의 종류에 따른 dpi가 정리되어 있다.

dpi	밀도	pixel	device[2]
ldpi (Low)	120dpi	0.75px	-
mdpi (Medium)	160dpi	1px	Galaxy Tab 10, Surface
hdpi (High)	240dpi	1.5px	Android One, Surface Pro 3
xhdpi (Extra)	320dpi	2px	Dell Venue 8, Surface Pro 4
xxhdpi (Extra Extra)	480dpi	3px	Google Pixel, LG G3
xxxhdpi (Extra Extra Extra)	640dpi	4px	Google Pixel XL, S7, S7 Edge, S8, S8+

Android SDK의 에뮬레이터 스킨에서 사용 가능한 다양한 화면구성과 기타 대표 해상도를 아래 표에 정리하였다[1].

	저밀도(120), *ldpi*	중간 밀도(160), *mdpi*	고밀도(240), *hdpi*	초고밀도(320), *xhdpi*
소형화면	QVGA (240x320)		480x640	
보통화면	WQVGA400 (240x400) WQVGA432 (240x432)	HVGA (320x480)	WVGA800 (480x800) WVGA854 (480x854) 600x1024	640x960
대형화면	WVGA800** (480x800) WVGA854** (480x854)	WVGA800* (480x800) WVGA854* (480x854) 600x1024		
초대형화면	1024x600	WXGA (1280x800) 1024x768 1280x768	1536x1152 1920x1152 1920x1200	2048x1536 2560x1536 2560x1600

sp는 Scale Independent Pixels의 약어이다. sp는 dp와 유사하지만 디바이스의 Font 크기설정에 따라 크기가 변경된다. 일반적으로 sp는 글꼴크기를 지정할 때 사용하는 것이 바람직하다.

dp와 px간의 변환 공식은 다음과 같다.

```
px = dp * (160/dpi) = dp * density
dp = px / (160/dpi) = px / density


ldpi의 density(pixel) = dp/density = 120/160(mdpi) = 0.75px
mdpi의 density(pixel) = dp/density = 160/160(mdpi) = 1.0px 로 구할 수 있다.
```

dpi와 density 구하는 방법

```
DisplayMetrics outMetrics = new DisplayMetrics();
getWindowManager().getDefaultDisplay().getMetrics(outMetrics);
int dpi = outMetrics.densityDpi;
float density =  outMetrics.density;
```

java 코드에서 dp를 px로 바꾸는 방법

```
public int dpToPixel(int dp){
    int px = TypedValue.applyDimension(TypedValue.COMPLEX_UNIT_DIP, DP,
            context.getResources().getDisplayMetrics());
}
```

일반적으로, 레이아웃 등의 UI에는 dp(dip)를 사용하는 것이 바람직하고, 글자 크기에는 sp를 사용하는 것이 바람직하다. px 단위는 사용하지 않는 것이 좋다.

실행되는 디바이스에 대한 크기를 pixel, DPI, Inch로 표현하는 프로그램을 작성

```java
public class MainActivity extends AppCompatActivity {
    @Override
    protected void onCreate(Bundle savedInstanceState) {
        super.onCreate(savedInstanceState);
        setContentView(R.layout.activity_main);

        DisplayMetrics displayMetrics = new DisplayMetrics();
        getWindowManager().getDefaultDisplay().getMetrics(displayMetrics);

        // pixel 화면 가로 크기
        float widthPixels = displayMetrics.widthPixels;
        float heightPixels = displayMetrics.heightPixels;

        DecimalFormat df = new DecimalFormat("#,###");

        TextView pix = (TextView) findViewById(R.id.textView11);
        pix.setText("Pixel :" + df.format(widthPixels) + " X " + df.format(heightPixels));

        // DPI 화면 가로 크기
        float widthDPI  = displayMetrics.xdpi;
        float heightDPI = displayMetrics.ydpi;

        TextView dpi = (TextView) findViewById(R.id.textView12);
        dpi.setText("DPI :" + df.format(widthDPI) + " X " + df.format(heightDPI));
        // Inch 화면 가로 크기
        float widthInch  = displayMetrics.widthPixels / displayMetrics.xdpi;
        float heightInch = displayMetrics.heightPixels / displayMetrics.ydpi;
```

```
            TextView inch = (TextView) findViewById(R.id.textView13);
            inch.setText("Inch :" + df.format(widthInch) + " X " +
                        df.format(heightInch));
    }
}
```

[실행 결과 : Pixel_XL_API_27]

Hello~ Y'su

Pixel :1,440 X 2,392

DPI :560 X 560

Inch :3 X 4

[실행 결과 : Nexus_5X_API_27]

Hello~ Y'su

Pixel :1,080 X 1,794

DPI :420 X 420

Inch :3 X 4

[실행 결과 : Nexus_4_API_25]

Hello~ Y'su

Pixel :768 X 1,184

DPI :320 X 320

Inch :2 X 4

참 · 고 · 자 · 료

[1]　mdpi, hdpi, xhdpi, xxhdpi, xxxhdpi 개념, https://developer.android.com/guide/practices/screens_support.html?hl=ko

[2]　안드로이드 해상도별 지원 기기 정보, https://material.io/devices/

ImageViewer 위젯 사용해보기

이번 장에서는 이미지를 보여주는 ImageViewer 위젯을 이해하고 실습한다.

6.1 ImageViewe 위젯 사용

ImageViewer 사용법을 익힌다.

안드로이드 앱의 대부분은 텍스트와 이미지로 구성되어 있다. 이미지를 표시하기 위해 ImageView 위젯을 사용한다. [그림 6-1]처럼 ImageView는 android.view.View 클래스에서 상속되었기 때문에, View 클래스에서 사용되는 기능을 그대로 사용할 수 있다.

ImageView

```
public class ImageView
extends View
```

java.lang.Object
  ↳ android.view.View
      ↳ android.widget.ImageView

[그림 6-1] ImageView 상속도

ImageView 위젯을 사용하기 위해, 먼저 이미지(Image)를 /res/Drawable에 이미지를 추가한다. 이미지를 추가할 때 주의할 점이 있다.

- 이미지 이름은 한글이 오면 안 된다. (한글.jpg)
- 숫자가 맨 앞에 오면 안 된다. (2abc.jpg)

- 이름 사이에 공백이 오면 안 된다. (a b c.jpg)
- 이름에 대문자가 들어가면 안 된다. (ABc.jpg)
- 이미지의 크기를 조정하여 메모리에 최적화 시켜야 오류가 적다.

/res/Drawable에 com.jpg 이미지를 추가하는 과정은 다음과 같다. 원본 파일인 com.jpg 파일이 위치한 곳에서 "복사하기"를 선택하여 /res/Drawable 위치에서 "붙여넣기(Paste)" 를 한다.

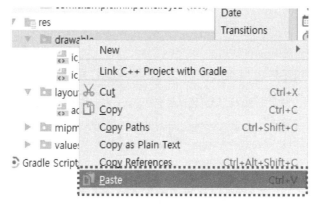

[그림 6-2] 복사한 그림을 붙여넣기

[그림 6-3]에서 그림을 복사하기 전에 복사될 이름을 먼저 묻고 있다. 이름에 오류가 없는 지 한 번 더 확인해야 한다.

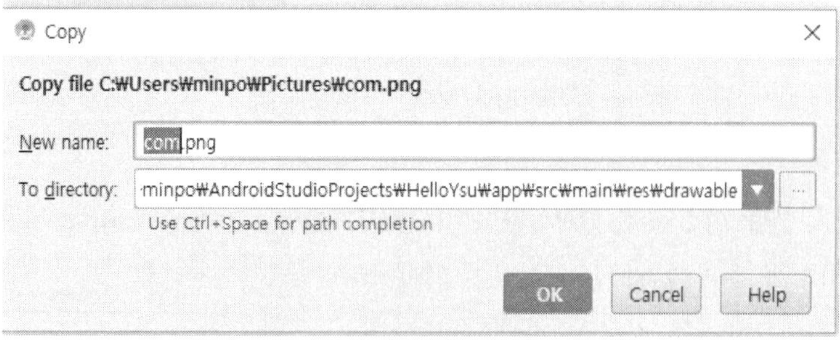

[그림 6-3] 그림 이름 확인하기

[그림 6-4]에서 /res/drawable에 com.png가 복사된 것을 확인할 수 있다.

[그림 6-4] /res/drawable에 복사

다음 단계는 [그림 6-5]처럼 ImageView 위젯을 끌어와서 배치시킨다.

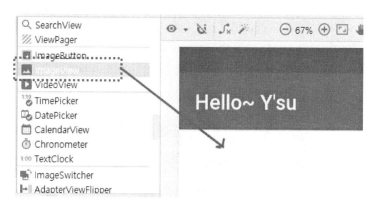

[그림 6-5] ImageView 위젯 끌어다놓기(drag)

ImageView를 배치시키면 자동으로 [그림 6-6]과 같은 화면이 팝업(pop-up) 된다.

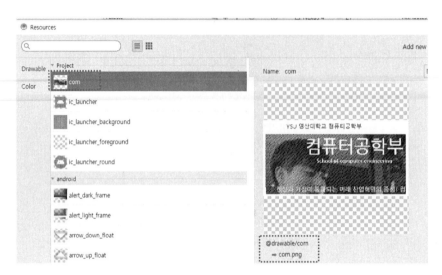

[그림 6-6] 리소스(Resource) 선택 화면

그림을 선택한 후, 배치된 결과는 [그림 6-7]과 같다.

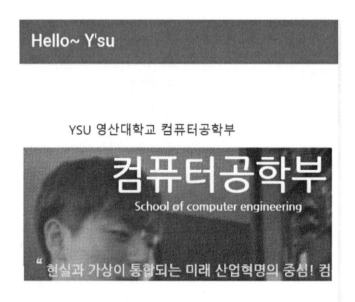

[그림 6-7] 이미지 배치 결과

[그림 6-7]을 배치한 activity_main.xml의 결과는 다음과 같다.

```
<ImageView
        android:id="@+id/imageView"
        android:layout_width="384dp"
        android:layout_height="315dp"
        app:srcCompat="@drawable/com"
        tools:layout_editor_absoluteX="0dp"
        tools:layout_editor_absoluteY="0dp"
/>
```

6.2 코드에서 Image를 변경해보기

학습목표

ImageView에 표시되는 이미지를 코드에서 변경하는 절차를 살펴보자.

먼저 findViewById() 함수를 사용하여 ImageView에 대한 참조(reference)를 얻는다. 얻어온 참조를 사용하여 setImageResource()를 호출하여 이미지를 변경한다.

findViewById()에서 사용하는 R.id.imageView 값은 이미지를 포함하고 있는 틀(holder, 액자)의 ID 값을 의미한다. 그 틀에 배치할 이미지는 "com.jpg"를 의미하는 R.drawable.com 값이 된다.

```java
public class MainActivity extends AppCompatActivity {
    @Override
    protected void onCreate(Bundle savedInstanceState) {
        super.onCreate(savedInstanceState);
        setContentView(R.layout.activity_main);

        ImageView iv = (ImageView) findViewById(R.id.imageView);
        iv.setImageResource(R.drawable.com);
    }
}
```

6.3 모바일 액자 앱 구현하기

모바일 액자 앱의 기능은 여러 장의 사진을 다음(Next) 버튼을 눌러 다음 사진을 보여주고 이전(Prev) 버튼을 사용하여 이전 사진을 보여준다. 사진 5장을 준비하자. 항상 저작권에 주의하고 직접 촬영한 사진을 사용하는 것을 추천한다. 알씨(AlSee) 도구를 사용하여 이미지 크기를 동일하게 500×400 크기로 재조정하자.

사진 5장의 이름을 "com.png "second.png", "third.png", "fourth.png", "fifth.png"로 설정한다. 파일의 확장자는 jpg, png 모두 사용될 수 있다. 주의할 점은 사진의 용량이 너무 크면 에뮬레이터 실행 시, 메모리 부족으로 오류가 발생한다. 또한 이미지 파일의 이름을 지정할 때, 이름 규칙에 따라 지정해야 한다.

변환된 이미지 파일을 [그림 6-8]처럼 /res/drawable에 복사해 넣자.

[그림 6-8] /res/drawable에 사진 복사

[그림 6-9]처럼 복사된 그림에서 "com.png" 파일을 첫 번째 파일로 사용하여 ImageView 위젯을 사용하여 배치하자. 다음은 "이전 사진" 버튼과 "다음 사진" 버튼을 배치하자.

[그림 6-9] 첫 화면 배치 (2개의 Button 위젯, 1개의 ImageView 위젯)

다음 단계는 첫 화면에 배치된 "이전 사진" 버튼과 "다음 사진" 버튼에 대한 코드를 추가하자.

```java
public class MainActivity extends AppCompatActivity {
    @Override
    protected void onCreate(Bundle savedInstanceState) {
        super.onCreate(savedInstanceState);
        setContentView(R.layout.activity_main);

        //1개의 ImageView에 대한 참조 얻기
        ImageView iv = (ImageView) findViewById(R.id.imageView);

        //2개의 버튼에 대한 참조 얻기
        Button prev = (Button) findViewById(R.id.button);
        Button next = (Button) findViewById(R.id.button2);

        //2개의 버튼에 대한 이벤트 코드 추가하기
        prev.setOnClickListener(new View.OnClickListener() {
            @Override
            public void onClick(View view) {

            }
        });

        next.setOnClickListener(new View.OnClickListener() {
            @Override
            public void onClick(View view) {

            }
        });
    }
}
```

다음 단계는 "다음 버튼"을 선택하면 현재의 "com.png"에서 "second.png"로 넘어가는 프로그램을 작성해보자.

"다음 버튼"이 선택되면 실행되는 "next.setOnClickListener()"에서 다음 사진을 보여주는 코드를 넣는다. 아래의 코드처럼 "iv.setImageResource(R.drawable.second);"를 추가한다. "R.drawable.second"는 두 번째 사진을 의미한다. 코드를 모두 입력하고 나면, iv 변수에 오류가 발생한다.

```
ImageView iv = (ImageView) findViewById(R.id.imageView);

next.setOnClickListener(new View.OnClickListener() {
    @Override
    public void onClick(View view) {
        iv.setImageResource(R.drawable.second);
    }
});
```

오류가 발생하는 원인은 iv 변수는 onCreate() 함수에서 정의되었는데 onCreate() 함수가 실행 종료가 되면 iv 변수는 메모리에서 사라지게 된다. iv 변수가 사라진 뒤에 "다음 버튼"이 선택되어 "next.setOnClickListener()"가 호출되면 이미 사라진 iv 변수를 호출하게 된다.

오류를 해결하는 방법은 iv 변수를 선언(declare)할 때, final 키워드를 사용한다. final 키워드가 변수 앞에 있으면 iv 값은 더 이상 변경할 수 없는 "상수"가 된다. 상수가 되면 iv 변수는 프로그램이 종료할 때까지 존재하는 변수로 속성이 된다. 다음과 같이 코드를 변경한다.

```
public class MainActivity extends AppCompatActivity {
    @Override
    protected void onCreate(Bundle savedInstanceState) {
        super.onCreate(savedInstanceState);
        setContentView(R.layout.activity_main);

        final ImageView iv = (ImageView) findViewById(R.id.imageView);

        Button prev = (Button) findViewById(R.id.button);
        Button next = (Button) findViewById(R.id.button2);

        prev.setOnClickListener(new View.OnClickListener() {
            @Override
            public void onClick(View view) {

            }
        });

        next.setOnClickListener(new View.OnClickListener() {
            @Override
            public void onClick(View view) {
                iv.setImageResource(R.drawable.second);

            }
        });
    }
}
```

다음 단계는 "다음 버튼"을 선택하면 차례대로 사진을 보여주는 코드를 추가하자.

[그림 6-10]처럼 실제에서는 com.png -> second.png -> third.png -> fourth.png -> fifth.png 순서로 사진이 보여지길 바란다. 안드로이드에서는 각각의 사진을 하나의 상태로 표현한다. com.png는 상태 '0', second.png는 상태 '1', third.png는 상태 '2', fourth.png는 상태 '3', fifth.png는 상태 '4'로 매칭한다. 즉, 안드로이드 프로그래밍에서

는 0 -〉 1 -〉 2 -〉 3 -〉 4 -〉 5 순서로 상태가 변경된다. 이 상태 값을 저장하는 변수를 status 로 선언한다. 변수란 컴퓨터 프로그램이 변하는 임시 값을 저장하는 컴퓨터 메모리 장소로 정의된다.

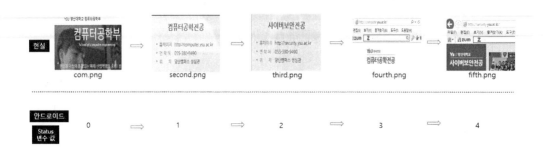

[그림 6-10] 현실 세계의 사진 움직임을 컴퓨터 메모리에서의 사진 움직임으로 정의

"다음 사진"에 대한 코드를 [그림 6-10]에서 보여준다.

```java
public class MainActivity extends AppCompatActivity {
    int status = 0; //0 : 첫 번째 사진으로 설정

    @Override
    protected void onCreate(Bundle savedInstanceState) {
        super.onCreate(savedInstanceState);
        setContentView(R.layout.activity_main);

        final ImageView iv = (ImageView) findViewById(R.id.imageView);
        Button prev = (Button) findViewById(R.id.button);
        Button next = (Button) findViewById(R.id.button2);

        prev.setOnClickListener(new View.OnClickListener() {
            @Override
            public void onClick(View view) {

            }
        });
```

```
next.setOnClickListener(new View.OnClickListener() {
    @Override
    public void onClick(View view) {
        status = status + 1;
        if(status == 0) { //첫 번째 사진
            iv.setImageResource(R.drawable.com);
        } else if(status == 1) { //두 번째 사진
            iv.setImageResource(R.drawable.second);
        } else if(status == 2) { //세 번째 사진
            iv.setImageResource(R.drawable.third);
        } else if(status == 3) { //네 번째 사진
            iv.setImageResource(R.drawable.fourth);
        } else if(status == 4) { //다섯 번째 사진
            iv.setImageResource(R.drawable.fifth);
        }

    }
});
    }
}
```

[실행 결과]

첫 번째 사진   두 번째 사진

코딩된 프로그램을 실행하면, 사진을 차례대로 볼 수 있다. 하지만, 마지막 사진(다섯 번째 사진)에서 "다음 버튼"을 선택하면 마지막 사진만 계속 보인다. 즉, 0 → 1 → 2 → 3 → 4 상태에서 '4' 상태에서 다음 상태를 정의하지 않았기 때문이다. 마지막 사진에서 "다음 버튼"을 선택하면 첫 번째 사진으로 갈 수 있게 만들자. 즉, [그림 6-11]처럼 컴퓨터 메모리에서의 상태 변수인 status를 0 → 1 → 2 → 3 → 4 → 0 → 1 → ... 로 변경한다.

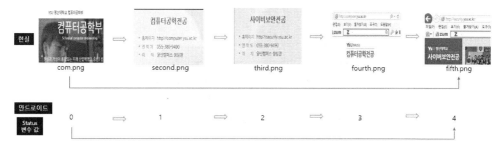

[그림 6-11] 마지막 사진에서 "다음 버튼"을 선택했을 때의 상태변화

```
public class MainActivity extends AppCompatActivity {
    int status = 0; //0 : 첫 번째 사진으로 설정

    @Override
    protected void onCreate(Bundle savedInstanceState) {
        super.onCreate(savedInstanceState);
        setContentView(R.layout.activity_main);

        final ImageView iv = (ImageView) findViewById(R.id.imageView);
        Button prev = (Button) findViewById(R.id.button);
        Button next = (Button) findViewById(R.id.button2);

        prev.setOnClickListener(new View.OnClickListener() {
            @Override
            public void onClick(View view) {

            }
        });

        next.setOnClickListener(new View.OnClickListener() {
            @Override
            public void onClick(View view) {
                status = status + 1;
                if(status == 5) status = 0; //마지막 사진이라면, 첫번째 사진으로
```

```
        if(status == 0) { //첫 번째 사진
            iv.setImageResource(R.drawable.com);
        } else if(status == 1) { //두 번째 사진
            iv.setImageResource(R.drawable.second);
        } else if(status == 2) { //세 번째 사진
            iv.setImageResource(R.drawable.third);
        } else if(status == 3) { //네 번째 사진
            iv.setImageResource(R.drawable.fourth);
        } else if(status == 4) { //다섯 번째 사진
            iv.setImageResource(R.drawable.fifth);
        }
    }
    });
    }
}
```

"다음 버튼"과 같은 방식으로 "이전 버튼"을 만들어 보자. "다음 버튼"처럼 상태 코드가 늘어나는 것이 아니라 감소하게 된다. 즉, [그림 6-12]처럼 상태변수인 status가 0 → 4 → 3 → 2 → 1 → 0 → 4 → …로 상태가 변경된다.

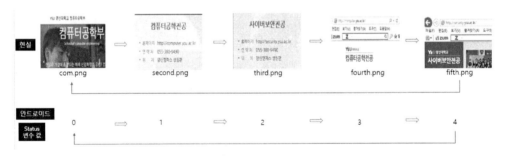

[그림 6-12] 첫 번째 사진에서 "이전 버튼"을 선택했을 때의 상태변화

구현된 코드는 다음과 같다.

```java
public class MainActivity extends AppCompatActivity {
    int status = 0; //0 : 첫 번째 사진으로 설정

    @Override
    protected void onCreate(Bundle savedInstanceState) {
        super.onCreate(savedInstanceState);
        setContentView(R.layout.activity_main);

        final ImageView iv = (ImageView) findViewById(R.id.imageView);
        Button prev = (Button) findViewById(R.id.button);
        Button next = (Button) findViewById(R.id.button2);

        prev.setOnClickListener(new View.OnClickListener() {
            @Override
            public void onClick(View view) {
                status = status - 1;
                if(status == -1) status = 4; //마지막 사진이라면, 첫번째 사진으로

                if(status == 0) { //첫 번째 사진
                    iv.setImageResource(R.drawable.com);
                } else if(status == 1) { //두 번째 사진
                    iv.setImageResource(R.drawable.second);
                } else if(status == 2) { //세 번째 사진
                    iv.setImageResource(R.drawable.third);
                } else if(status == 3) { //네 번째 사진
                    iv.setImageResource(R.drawable.fourth);
                } else if(status == 4) { //다섯 번째 사진
                    iv.setImageResource(R.drawable.fifth);
                }
            }
        });

        next.setOnClickListener(new View.OnClickListener() {
            @Override
            public void onClick(View view) {
```

```
status = status + 1;
if(status == 5) status = 0; //마지막 사진이라면, 첫번째 사진으로

if(status == 0) { //첫 번째 사진
    iv.setImageResource(R.drawable.com);
} else if(status == 1) { //두 번째 사진
    iv.setImageResource(R.drawable.second);
} else if(status == 2) { //세 번째 사진
    iv.setImageResource(R.drawable.third);
} else if(status == 3) { //네 번째 사진
    iv.setImageResource(R.drawable.fourth);
} else if(status == 4) { //다섯 번째 사진
    iv.setImageResource(R.drawable.fifth);
}
        }
    });
    }
}
```

참·고·자·료

[1]   안드로이드 ImageView 상속도,

https://developer.android.com/reference/android/ widget/ImageView.html

안드로이드 사운드 응용해보기

이번 장에서는 안드로이드에서의 사운드를 이해하고 응용 프로그램을 만든다.

안드로이드 디바이스에서 사운드(소리)를 재생하고 관리하는 방법은 두 가지가 있다. 첫 번째는 MediaPlayer를 클래스를 사용하는 방법이다. 두 번재는 SoundPool 클래스를 이용하는 방법이다.

MediaPlayer로 안드로이드 사운드 프로그램 만들기

학습목표

안드로이드 MediaPlayer 클래스를 이해한다.

MediaPlayer는 [그림 7-1]과 같이 많은 다양한 상태 (Idle, Initialized, Prepared, Preparing, Started, Stopped, Paused, PlaybackCompleted)를 가지고 있다[1]. 즉, 여러분이 안드로이드 디바이스에서 소리를 나오게 하면 위의 다양한 상태를 바꾸어 가면서 관리를 하게 된다. 상태에 맞지 않는 함수(Method)를 호출하게 되면 IllegalStateException이 발생된다.

MediaPlayer는 다루는 미디어 파일들이 용량이 크기 때문에, 미디어 파일을 메모리에서 관리하는 버퍼 관련 콜백(Callback)들이 많다.

MediaPlayer를 사용하여 외부 URL에서 사운드를 스트리밍(Streaming) 하거나 재생 중에 화면이 어두워지거나 꺼지는 것을 막기 위해 두 가지 권한을 AndroidManifest.xml에 추가한다.

```
<uses-permission android:name=" android.permission.INTERNET " />
<uses-permission android:name=" android.permission.WAKE_LOCK " />
```

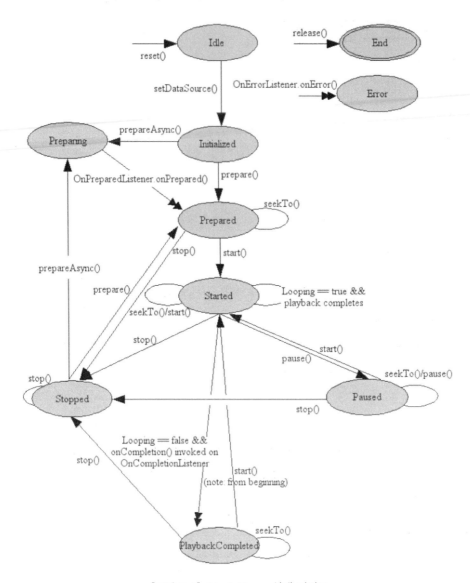

[그림 7-1] MediaPlayer 상태 전이도

MediaPlayer를 이용하여 소리를 재생하는 프로그램을 작성해보자.

먼저, 재생할 소리를 /res/raw 폴더에 MP3 파일을 복사해 넣자. image와 마찬가지로 파일의 이름에 주의해야 한다.

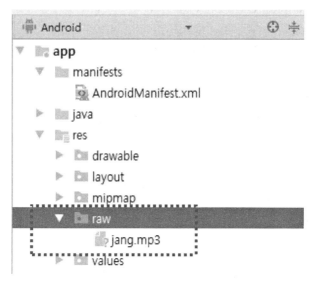

[그림 7-2] mp3 파일을 /res/raw에 복사하기

복사한 "jang.mp3" 파일을 재생하기 위해서 MediaPlayer 클래스를 사용한다. MediaPlayer 객체를 생성하고 /res/raw 폴더에 있는 파일의 resource id를 인수로 지정한다.

다음 단계는 [그림 7-3]처럼 3개의 버튼을 생성한다. 각각의 버튼 이름은 "Play", "Pause", "Stop"이다.

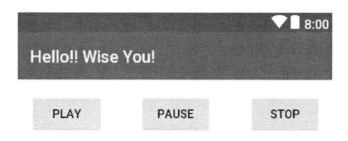

[그림 7-3] 3개의 버튼 생성

"Play" 버튼의 id는 button9, "Pause" 버튼의 id는 button10, "Stop" 버튼의 id는 button11 이다. 각 버튼의 이벤트 리스너를 등록하자.

```
protected void onCreate(Bundle savedInstanceState) {
        super.onCreate(savedInstanceState);
        setContentView(R.layout.activity_main);

        Button play = (Button) findViewById(R.id.button9);
        Button pause = (Button) findViewById(R.id.button10);
        Button stop = (Button) findViewById(R.id.button11);

        play.setOnClickListener(new View.OnClickListener() {
            @Override
            public void onClick(View view) {

            }
        });

        pause.setOnClickListener(new View.OnClickListener() {
            @Override
            public void onClick(View view) {

            }
        });

        stop.setOnClickListener(new View.OnClickListener() {
            @Override
            public void onClick(View view) {

            }
        });
```

다음 단계는 mp3를 재생하기 위한 MediaPlayer를 생성한다.

```
mp = MediaPlayer.create(MainActivity.this, R.raw.jang);
```

MediaPlay 객체를 생성 후에 [그림 7-1]처럼 "Idle" 상태와 "Initialize" 상태를 통과하고 "stopped" 상태로 바로 가기위해, stop() 함수를 create() 함수 호출 후에 사용한다.

```
mp = MediaPlayer.create(MainActivity.this, R.raw.jang);
mp.stop();
```

[그림 7-1]처럼 "stopped" 상태에서 "Prepared" 상태로 가기 위해서 prepare() 함수를 사용한다. 다음의 예는 "stopped" 상태에서 "Prepared" 상태로 가서 "Started"에서 음악이 재생되는 코드이다. 아래의 코드는 버튼 상태와는 상관없이 재생된다.

```
MediaPlayer mp3;

    @Override
    protected void onCreate(Bundle savedInstanceState) {
        super.onCreate(savedInstanceState);
        setContentView(R.layout.activity_main);

        mp3 = MediaPlayer.create(MainActivity.this, R.raw.jang);
        mp3.stop();
        try {
            mp3.prepare();
        } catch (IOException e) {

        }
        mp3.start();


        Button play = (Button) findViewById(R.id.button9);
        Button pause = (Button) findViewById(R.id.button10);
        Button stop = (Button) findViewById(R.id.button11);

        play.setOnClickListener(new View.OnClickListener() {
            @Override
            public void onClick(View view) {

            }
        });

        pause.setOnClickListener(new View.OnClickListener() {
            @Override
            public void onClick(View view) {
```

```
            }
        });

        stop.setOnClickListener(new View.OnClickListener() {
            @Override
            public void onClick(View view) {


            }
        });
```

다음 단계는 "Stopped" 상태에서 "play" 버튼을 누르면 재생이 되고 "stop" 버튼을 누르면
재생이 멈추게 한다. 다시 "play" 버튼을 누르면 재생이 처음부터 된다.

```
MediaPlayer mp3;

    @Override
    protected void onCreate(Bundle savedInstanceState) {
        super.onCreate(savedInstanceState);
        setContentView(R.layout.activity_main);

        mp3 = MediaPlayer.create(MainActivity.this, R.raw.jang);
        mp3.stop();

        Button play = (Button) findViewById(R.id.button9);
        Button pause = (Button) findViewById(R.id.button10);
        Button stop = (Button) findViewById(R.id.button11);

        play.setOnClickListener(new View.OnClickListener() {
            @Override
            public void onClick(View view) {
                try {
                    mp3.prepare();
                } catch (IOException e) {
```

```
            }
            mp3.start();
        }
    });

    pause.setOnClickListener(new View.OnClickListener() {
        @Override
        public void onClick(View view) {

        }
    });

    stop.setOnClickListener(new View.OnClickListener() {
        @Override
        public void onClick(View view) {
            mp3.stop();
        }
    });
```

현재 단계에서 작성된 코드는 "play" 버튼을 다시 누르면 앱이 죽어버린다. [그림 7-1]에서
보듯이, 현재 mp3가 현재 play 중인 "Started" 상태인데, "Prepared" 상태를 바로 호출하였
기 때문이다. 반드시 "Stopped" 상태로 가서 "Prepared" 상태로 진입을 해야 한다.

이를 위해 mp3가 현재 음악을 재생 중인 것을 확인하는 "isPlaying()" 함수를 사용한다.
사용자에게 현재 음악이 재생 중이라는 것을 알리기 위해 버튼의 텍스트를 "재생중입니
다."로 변경하고 "setClickable()" 함수를 사용하여 버튼을 click하지 못하게 한다. "stop"
버튼에서는 현재 음악이 재생 중 일때만 "stop()" 함수를 실행할 수 있게 한다.

```
    @Override
    protected void onCreate(Bundle savedInstanceState) {
        super.onCreate(savedInstanceState);
        setContentView(R.layout.activity_main);
```

```
MediaPlayer mp3;

        mp3 = MediaPlayer.create(MainActivity.this, R.raw.jang);
        mp3.stop();

        final Button play = (Button) findViewById(R.id.button9);
        Button pause = (Button) findViewById(R.id.button10);
        final Button stop = (Button) findViewById(R.id.button11);
        stop.setClickable(false);

        play.setOnClickListener(new View.OnClickListener() {
            @Override
            public void onClick(View view) {
                if(!mp3.isPlaying()) {
                    try {
                        mp3.prepare();
                    } catch (IOException e) {

                    }
                    mp3.start();
                    play.setText("재생중입니다.");
                    play.setClickable(false);
                    stop.setClickable(true);
                }
            }
        });

        pause.setOnClickListener(new View.OnClickListener() {
            @Override
            public void onClick(View view) {

            }
        });

        stop.setOnClickListener(new View.OnClickListener() {
            @Override
            public void onClick(View view) {
                if(mp3.isPlaying()) {
```

```
                            mp3.stop();
                            play.setText("play");
                            play.setClickable(true);
                            stop.setClickable(false);
                    }
                }
            });
```

다음 단계는 "pause" 기능을 구현한다. [그림 7-1]의 상태도에서 pause() 함수를 호출하면 "Started" 상태에서 "Pause" 상태로 전이된다. 다시 "Started" 상태로 전이되기 위해서는 start() 함수를 사용한다. MediaPlayer의 getCurrentPosition() 함수를 이용하여 원하는 위치로 이동하여도 된다. getCurrentPosition() 함수를 사용하지 않아도 재생이 일시 멈춘 위치에서 다시 시작할 수 있다.

```
MediaPlayer mp3;
    int cuPos = 0;
    @Override
    protected void onCreate(Bundle savedInstanceState) {
        super.onCreate(savedInstanceState);
        setContentView(R.layout.activity_main);

        mp3 = MediaPlayer.create(MainActivity.this, R.raw.jang);
        mp3.stop();

        final Button play = (Button) findViewById(R.id.button9);
        final Button pause = (Button) findViewById(R.id.button10);
        final Button stop = (Button) findViewById(R.id.button11);
        stop.setClickable(false);

        play.setOnClickListener(new View.OnClickListener() {
            @Override
            public void onClick(View view) {
                if(!mp3.isPlaying()) {
```

```
                    try {
                        mp3.prepare();
                    } catch (IOException e) {

                    }
                    mp3.start();
                    play.setText("playing...");
                    play.setClickable(false);
                    stop.setClickable(true);
                }
            }
        });

        pause.setOnClickListener(new View.OnClickListener() {
            @Override
            public void onClick(View view) {
                if(mp3.isPlaying()) {
                    cuPos = mp3.getCurrentPosition();
                    mp3.pause();
                    pause.setText("resume");
                } else if(mp3 != null && !mp3.isPlaying()){
                    mp3.seekTo(cuPos);
                    mp3.start();
                    pause.setText("pause");
                    Toast.makeText(MainActivity.this, cuPos + "에서 다시 시작
합니다.", Toast.LENGTH_SHORT).show();
                }
            }
        });

        stop.setOnClickListener(new View.OnClickListener() {
            @Override
            public void onClick(View view) {
                //if(mp3.isPlaying()) {
                    mp3.stop();
                    play.setText("play");
                    pause.setText("pause");
```

```
                    play.setClickable(true);
                    stop.setClickable(false);
                //}
            }
        });
```

[실행 화면]

앞의 예제에서 mp3 파일의 재생, 멈춤, 일시 멈춤 기능을 구현해 보았다. 이번 예제에서는 MediaPlayer를 이용하여 인터넷으로 연결하여 동영상을 볼 수 있는 동영상 플레이어를 구현해보자. 오디오 재생과 거의 유사한 방법을 사용합니다. MediaPlayer 클래스보다 향상된 VideoView 클래스를 이용할 수 있다.

MediaPlayer가 Play할 수 있는 프로토콜(형식)은 "RTSP", "HTTP/HTTPS Progressive Streaming", "HTTP/HTTPS Live Streaming(HLS", "MPEG-2 TS", "Protocolversion 3(Android 4.0 & above)", "Protocol version 2(Android 3.X)", "3.0 버전 이하는 지원 안됨"이다. 오픈소스를 사용하여 좀더 세련되게 만들 수도 있다[2].

동영상을 표시할 스크린이 필요하기 때문에 SurfaceView를 스크린으로 사용한다. SurfaceView가 생성되는데 시간이 필요하기 때문으로 자동으로 동영상 파일을 로딩하려면 이벤트 함수를 사용해야 한다.

SurfaceView의 클래스 계층도는 [그림 7-4]와 같다[3].

SurfaceView

public class SurfaceView

extends View

java.lang.Object

    ↳ android.view.View

        ↳ android.view.SurfaceView

[그림 7-4] SurfaceView 계층도

Android 응용프로그램의 View는 GDI(Graphic Device Interface) Thread를 통해 Surface 에 그려진다. View에 동영상 또는 카메라 프리뷰와 같이 화면에 그려지는(drawing) 양이 매우 많거나 화면의 변화가 크다면 SurfaceView를 사용해야 한다. SurfaceView는 GDI Thread에 그려지지 않고 다른 Thread에 그려지게 된다. 즉, 현재의 View에 구멍 (Punching)을 내서 특정 영역을 보이게 하는 방식이다.

Surface는 그래픽 버퍼(Graphic Buffer)입니다. SurfaceView에 그림을 그리는 작업은 SurfaceHolder라고 불리는 콜백(Callback) 함수가 합니다. 콜백 함수는 사용자는 정의만 하고 그 함수를 호출하는 주체는 운영체제(시스템)이다.

먼저, [그림 7-5]처럼 MediaPlayer에는 화면이 포함되지 않기 때문에 동영상을 화면에 표 현하기 위해 SurfaceView 위젯을 레이아웃에 추가하자.

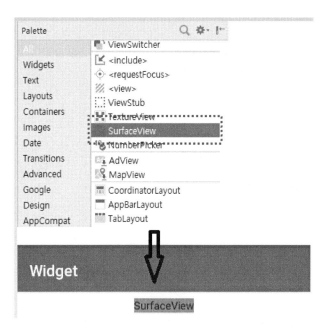

[그림 7-5] Surface Widge 추가

앞의 예제처럼, "play", "pause", "stop" 버튼을 추가하고 3개의 버튼에 대한 이벤트 리스너
도 등록하자. SurfaceView의 기본 코드까지 포함한 코드는 다음과 같다.

```java
public class MainActivity extends AppCompatActivity implements
SurfaceHolder.Callback{
    SurfaceView sv;
    SurfaceHolder sufaceHolder;
    MediaPlayer mediaPlayer;
    Button start, stop, pause;

    @Override
    protected void onCreate(Bundle savedInstanceState) {
        super.onCreate(savedInstanceState);
        setContentView(R.layout.activity_main);

        if(mediaPlayer == null) {
            mediaPlayer = new MediaPlayer();
        } else {
            mediaPlayer.reset();
        }
```

```
        sv = (SurfaceView) findViewById((R.id.surfaceView));
        sufaceHolder = sv.getHolder();
        sufaceHolder.addCallback(this);



        start = (Button)findViewById(R.id.button);
        start.setText("영상이 없습니다.");
        //start.setClickable(false);

        pause = (Button)findViewById(R.id.button2);
        pause.setText("영상이 없습니다.");
        pause.setClickable(false);

        stop = (Button)findViewById(R.id.button3);
        stop.setText("영상이 없습니다.");
        stop.setClickable(false);

        start.setOnClickListener(new View.OnClickListener() {
            @Override
            public void onClick(View view) {
                start.setText("onclick");
                if(mediaPlayer == null) {
                    mediaPlayer = new MediaPlayer();
                } else {
                    mediaPlayer.reset();
                }
                try {
                    //local에 접근
                    //Uri uri = Uri.parse("android.resource://" +
getPackageName() + "/raw/a");

                    //internet에 접근
                    //영산대 사이버보안 전공 접근
                    //https://www.youtube.com/embed/DEPIQ6rXemY
                    Uri uri =
Uri.parse("https://www.youtube.com/embed/DEPIQ6rXemY");
                    mediaPlayer.setDataSource(MainActivity.this, uri);
                    mediaPlayer.setDisplay(sufaceHolder); //Surface 화면 호출
                    mediaPlayer.prepare(); //관련 영상 불러오기(Load)
                    mediaPlayer.start();
                } catch (IOException e) {
```

```
                }
            }
        });

        pause.setOnClickListener(new View.OnClickListener() {
            @Override
            public void onClick(View view) {

            }
        });
        stop.setOnClickListener(new View.OnClickListener() {
            @Override
            public void onClick(View view) {

            }
        });
        /*Button start = (Button)findViewById(R.id.buttonStart);
        start.setOnClickListener(new View.OnClickListener() {
            @Override
            public void onClick(View view) {
                Intent is = new Intent(MainActivity.this, SubActivity.class);
                startActivity(is);
            }
        });*/
    }

    @Override
    protected void onDestroy() {
        super.onDestroy();
        if(mediaPlayer != null) {
            mediaPlayer.release();
        }
    }
    @Override
    public void surfaceCreated(SurfaceHolder surfaceHolder) {
        //Surface가 처음 만들어질 때,

        try {
            //local에 접근
            Uri uri = Uri.parse("android.resource://" + getPackageName() +
"/raw/a");
```

```
                //internet에 접근
                //영산대 사이버보안 전공 접근
                //https://www.youtube.com/embed/DEPIQ6rXemY
                //Uri uri =
Uri.parse("https://www.youtube.com/embed/DEPIQ6rXemY");
                mediaPlayer.setDataSource(this, uri);
                mediaPlayer.setDisplay(surfaceHolder); //Surface 화면 호출
                mediaPlayer.prepare(); //관련 영상 불러오기(Load)
                mediaPlayer.start();

                start.setText("suface에서.....");
                mediaPlayer.setOnCompletionListener(new
MediaPlayer.OnCompletionListener() {
                    @Override
                    public void onCompletion(MediaPlayer mediaPlayer) {
                        start.setText("Play");
                        pause.setText("Pause");
                        stop.setText("Stop");

                        mediaPlayer.start();
                    }
                });
            } catch (Exception e) {

            }
        }

    @Override
    public void surfaceChanged(SurfaceHolder surfaceHolder, int i, int i1, int
i2) {

        }

    @Override
    public void surfaceDestroyed(SurfaceHolder surfaceHolder) {

        }
}
```

[실행 결과]

해당 동영상은 저자의 연구실 천장 부분을 약 4초 정도 촬영한 영상이다.

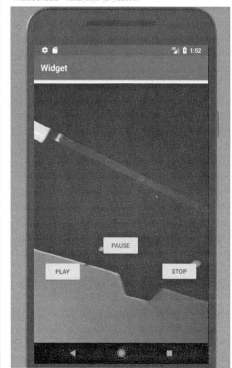

SoundPool 로 안드로이드 사운드 프로그램 만들기

학습목표

안드로이드 SoundPool 클래스를 이해한다.

SoundPool 클래스를 사용하기 위한 절차는 객체를 먼저 생성하고 리소스(음악파일)를 메모리에 로드해서 실행을 한다.

SoundPool pool = new SoundPool(최대 스트림 수, 오디오 스트링 타입, 샘플링 품질);

- 최대 스트림 수 : 동시에 재생이 가능한 최대 스트림 개수

- 오디오 스트링 타입 : STREM_MUSIC이 일반적임

- 샘플링 품질 : 0을 일반적으로 사용함

예) pool = new SoundPool(1, AudioManager.STREAM_MUSIC, 0);

AudioManager

```
public class AudioManager
extends Object
```

java.lang.Object
 └ android.media.AudioManager

다음 단계는 load() 함수를 사용하여 실제 리소스(Resource) 파일을 가져온다.

```
int pool = pool.load(Context, Resource ID, Priority);
- Context : 현재 실행 중인 View가 아닌 Activity 값을 넣어줌
- Resource ID : 로드할 Sound ID
- 우선권 : 1을 넣어줌


예) poolhandle = pool.load(this, R.raw.jang, 1);
```

다음 단계는 play() 함수를 사용하여 소리를 재생하는 방법이다.

```
pool.play(실행할 Resource ID, 왼쪽 볼륨, 오른쪽 볼륨, 재생 우선 순위, 반복여부,
속도);
예)
- Context : 현재 실행 중인 View가 아닌 Activity 값을 넣어줌
- Resource ID : 로드할 Sound ID
- 우선권 : 1을 넣어줌


예)
- 소리 듣기(일반)
  pool.play(poolhandle, 1, 1, 0, 0, 1);


- 볼륨 1/2 줄이기
  pool.play(poolhandle, 0.5f, 0.5f, 0, 0, 1);


- 2배 속도 듣기
  pool.play(poolhandle, 1, 1, 0, 0, 2);
```

- 1/2배 속도 듣기

  pool.play(poolhandle, 1, 1, 0, 0, 0.5f);

- 오른 쪽 듣기

  pool.play(poolhandle, 0, 1, 0, 0, 1);

- 왼쪽 듣기

  pool.play(poolhandle, 1, 0, 0, 0, 1);

SoundPool의 기본 예제를 다음 코드를 참고하여 만들어보자.

```java
public class MainActivity extends AppCompatActivity {
    SoundPool pool;
    int poolhandle;

    MediaPlayer mp;

    @Override
    protected void onCreate(Bundle savedInstanceState) {
        super.onCreate(savedInstanceState);
        setContentView(R.layout.activity_main);

        //Media Player
        //mp = new MediaPlayer();
        mp = MediaPlayer.create(MainActivity.this, R.raw.jang);
        mp.stop();

        //재생시간이 짧은 효과음등을 재생할 수 있음 (재생시간이 긴 배경음악등은
MediaPlayer을 이용)

        //SoundPool 객체 생성
        pool = new SoundPool(1, AudioManager.STREAM_MUSIC, 0);
        pool.setOnLoadCompleteListener(new SoundPool.OnLoadCompleteListener() {
            @Override
```

```
        public void onLoadComplete(SoundPool soundPool, int i, int i1) {
            // pool.play(poolhandle, 1, 1, 0, 0, 1);


        }
    });
    //handle 얻기
    poolhandle = pool.load(this, R.raw.jang, 1);

    Button b1 = (Button) findViewById(R.id.button);
    b1.setOnClickListener(new View.OnClickListener() {
        @Override
        public void onClick(View view) { // 소리 듣기(일반)
            pool.play(poolhandle, 1, 1, 0, 0, 1);
        }
    });
    Button b2 = (Button) findViewById(R.id.button2);
    b2.setOnClickListener(new View.OnClickListener() {
        @Override
        public void onClick(View view) { //볼륨 1/2 줄이기
            pool.play(poolhandle, 0.5f, 0.5f, 0, 0, 1);
        }
    });
    Button b3 = (Button) findViewById(R.id.button3);
    b3.setOnClickListener(new View.OnClickListener() {
        @Override
        public void onClick(View view) { //2배 속도 듣기
            pool.play(poolhandle, 1, 1, 0, 0, 2);
        }
    });
    Button b4 = (Button) findViewById(R.id.button4);
    b4.setOnClickListener(new View.OnClickListener() {
        @Override
        public void onClick(View view) { // 1/2배 속도 듣기
            pool.play(poolhandle, 1, 1, 0, 0, 0.5f);
        }
    });
```

```java
        Button b5 = (Button) findViewById(R.id.button5);
        b5.setOnClickListener(new View.OnClickListener() {
            @Override
            public void onClick(View view) { //오른 쪽 듣기
                pool.play(poolhandle, 0, 1, 0, 0, 1);
            }
        });
        Button b6 = (Button) findViewById(R.id.button6);
        b6.setOnClickListener(new View.OnClickListener() {
            @Override
            public void onClick(View view) { //왼쪽 듣기
                pool.play(poolhandle, 1, 0, 0, 0, 1);
            }
        });


        Button b7 = (Button) findViewById(R.id.button7);
        b7.setOnClickListener(new View.OnClickListener() {
            @Override
            public void onClick(View view) { //왼쪽 듣기
                try {
                    mp.prepare();
                } catch (IOException e) {

                }
                mp.setVolume(0, 1);
                mp.start();
            }
        });
        Button b8 = (Button) findViewById(R.id.button8);
        b8.setOnClickListener(new View.OnClickListener() {
            @Override
            public void onClick(View view) { //왼쪽 듣기
                mp.stop();
            }
        });

    }
}
```

[실행 결과]

Hello!! Wise You!

저의 email은 minpo@ysu.ac.kr입

일반	오른쪽 듣기
1/2소리	왼쪽 듣기
2배	1/2배

MEDIA PLAY   STOP

[1]   MediaPlayer Class 작동 방법, https://developer.android.com/reference/android/
      media/MediaPlayer.html

[2]   좀 더 세련된 Audio, Media 제어를 위한 ExoPlayer,
      https://developer.android.com/guide/topics/media/exoplayer.html

[3]   Android SurfaceView, https://developer.android.com/reference/android/view/
      SurfaceView.html

Sub Activity 만들기

이번 장에서는 화면 전환을 위한 프로그래밍 기법을 이해하고 화면 전환 응용 프로그램을 만든다.

안드로이드 디바이스에서 화면을 전환하기 위한 가장 기본적인 방법으로 Intent를 사용한다.

Intent를 활용하여 화면 전환하기

학습목표

안드로이드 화면전환을 하는 기법을 이해한다.

안드로이드의 한 화면에 많은 정보를 표현하는 것은 매우 어려운 일이다. 일반적으로 액티비티(Activity)라고 불리는 다양한 종류의 화면을 구성하여 필요할 때마다 구성된 각각의 화면을 호출한다. 각각의 화면으로 전환하기 위해 사용되는 것이 Intent 이다.

Intent는 액티비티 등의 화면 전환이 필요할 때 사용되고 메시지를 전달할 수 있는 중간 역할을 한다. Intent를 사용하는 대표적인 사례[1]는 다음과 같다.

- 액티비티를 시작하기 위해 사용

Activity는 앱 안의 단말 화면을 나타낸다. Activity의 새 인스턴스(instance)를 시작하기 위해 Intent를 startActivity()로 전달하는 것만으로 코드는 끝난다.
Intent는 시작할 Activity를 설명하고 모든 필수 데이터를 담고 있다.
Activity가 완료되었을 때 결과를 수신하려면, startActivityForResult()를 호출한다.
해당 결과는 onActivityResult() 콜백에서 변도의 Intent 객체로 수신한다.

- 안드로이드 서비스(Service)를 시작하기 위해 사용

안드로이드 Service는 사용자 인터페이스 없이 백그라운드(background)에서 작업을 수행하는 구성 요소이다. 서비스를 시작하여 일회성 작업을 수행하도록 하려면 (예: 파일 다운로드) Intent를 startService()에 전달한다. Intent는 시작할 서비스를 설명하고 모든 필수 데이터를 담고 있다.
서비스가 클라이언트-서버 인터페이스로 디자인된 경우에는 다른 구성 요소로부터 서비스에 바인드(bind)를 하기 위해 Intent를 bindService()에 전달한다.

- 안드로이드 브로드캐스트(broadcast) 전달을 하기 위해 사용

브로드캐스트는 안드로이드 디바이스 내의 모든 앱이 수신할 수 있는 메시지이다. 시스템은 여러 시스템 이벤트에 대해 다양한 브로드캐스트를 전달한다. 예를 들어 시스템이 부팅될 때 또는 기기가 변경되기 시작할 때 등이 해당된다. 다른 여러 앱에 브로드캐스트를 전달하려면 Intent를 sendBroadcast(), sendOrderedBroadcast() 또는 sendStickyBroadcast()에 전달한다.

이 교재에서는 첫 번째 사용 사례인 액티비티를 사용하는 방법에 대해서만 언급된다.

Intent는 두 가지 유형이 있다.

명시적 인텐트는 시작할 구성 요소를 이름으로 지정한다. (완전히 정규화된 클래스 이름) 시작하고자 하는 액티비티 또는 서비스의 클래스 이름을 알고 있기 때문에 명시적으로 사용할 수 있다. 명시적 Intent는 전환될 다음 화면 액티비트를 직접 코드에 적는 방법이다. 예를 들어, 사용자 작업에 응답하여 새 액티비티를 시작하거나 백그라운드에서 파일을 다운로드하기 위해 서비스를 시작하는 것 등이 여기에 해당됩니다.

"MainActivity.this"는 현재의 화면을 의미하고 "SubActivity.class"는 전환될 화면을 명시적으로 지정한다. 지정 후에 startActivity() 함수로 화면을 전환한다.

```
Intent intnet = new Intent(MainActivity.this, SubActivity.class);
startActivity(intent);
```

암시적 인텐트는 특정 구성 요소의 이름을 대지 않지만, 그 대신 수행할 일반적일 작업을 선언하여 또 다른 앱의 구성 요소가 이를 처리할 수 있도록 해준다. 예를 들어, 사용자에게 지도에 있는 한 위치를 표시해주고자 하는 경우, 암시적 인텐트를 사용하여 다른, 해당 기능을 갖춘 앱이 지정된 위치를 지도에 표시하도록 요청할 수 있다.
암시적 Intent는 전환될 화면을 직접 지정하지 않고 액션(Action)을 지정하여 사용한다[2].

암시적 인텐트를 생성하면 Android 시스템이 시작시킬 적절한 구성 요소를 찾는다. 이때 인텐트의 내용을 기기에 있는 다른 여러 앱의 매니페스트 파일에서 선언된 인텐트 필터와 비교하는 방법을 사용한다. 해당 인텐트와 일치하는 인텐트 필터가 있으면 시스템이 해당 구성 요소를 시작하고 이에 Intent 객체를 전달한다. 호환되는 인텐트 필터가 여러 개인 경우, 시스템은 대화상자를 표시하여 사용자가 어느 앱을 사용할지 직접 선택할 수 있게 한다.

인텐트 필터란 앱의 매니페스트 파일에 들어 있는 표현으로, 해당 구성 요소가 수신하고자 하는 인텐트의 유형을 나타낸 것이다. 예를 들어 액티비티에 대한 인텐트 필터를 선언하면 다른 여러 앱이 특정한 종류의 인텐트를 가지고 여러분의 액티비티를 직접 시작할 수 있다. 이와 마찬가지로, 액티비티에 대한 인텐트 필터를 전혀 선언하지 않으면 명시적 인텐트로만 시작할 수 있다.

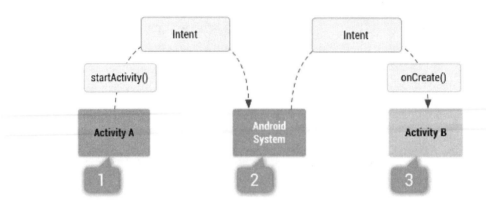

[그림 8-1] 암시적 인텐트로 액티비티 호출 방법[2]

[그림 8-1]은 암시적 인텐트로 액티비티를 호출하는 방법이다. "1"에서 액티비티 A가 작업 설명이 있는 Intent를 생성하여 이를 startActivity()에 전달한다. "2"에서 Android 시스템이 해당 인텐트와 일치하는 인텐트 필터를 찾아 모든 앱을 검색한다. 일치하는 항목을 찾으면, "3"에서 시스템이 일치하는 액티비티(액티비티 B)를 시작하기 위해 그 액티비티의 onCreate() 메서드를 호출하여 이를 Intent에 전달한다.

암시적 인텐트 예는 다음과 같다. startActivity()가 호출되면 시스템이 설치된 앱을 모두 살펴보고 이런 종류의 인텐트를 처리할 수 있는 앱이 어느 것인지 알아본다 (ACTION_SEND 작업을 포함하고 "text/plain" 데이터를 전달하는 인텐트). 이것을 처리할 수 있는 앱이 하나뿐이면, 해당 앱이 즉시 열리고 이 앱에 인텐트가 주어진다. 인텐트를 허용하는 액티비티가 여러 개인 경우, 시스템은 대화상자를 표시하여 사용자가 어느 앱을 사용할지 직접 선택할 수 있게 한다.

```
// Create the text message with a string
Intent sendIntent = new Intent();
sendIntent.setAction(Intent.ACTION_SEND);
sendIntent.putExtra(Intent.EXTRA_TEXT, textMessage);
sendIntent.setType("text/plain");
```

```
// Verify that the intent will resolve to an activity
if (sendIntent.resolveActivity(getPackageManager()) != null) {
    startActivity(sendIntent);
}
```

암시적 인텐트를 정상 작동 시키기 위해서는 반드시 AndroidManifest.xml 파일에서
〈intent-filter〉를 정의해야 한다. 다음에서 몇 가지 예를 제시한다.

```
<activity android:name="MainActivity">
    <!-- This activity is the main entry, should appear in app launcher -->
    <intent-filter>
        <action android:name="android.intent.action.MAIN" />
        <category android:name="android.intent.category.LAUNCHER" />
    </intent-filter>
</activity>

<activity android:name="ShareActivity">
    <!-- This activity handles "SEND" actions with text data -->
    <intent-filter>
        <action android:name="android.intent.action.SEND"/>
        <category android:name="android.intent.category.DEFAULT"/>
        <data android:mimeType="text/plain"/>
    </intent-filter>
    <!-- This activity also handles "SEND" and "SEND_MULTIPLE" with media data
-->
    <intent-filter>
        <action android:name="android.intent.action.SEND"/>
        <action android:name="android.intent.action.SEND_MULTIPLE"/>
        <category android:name="android.intent.category.DEFAULT"/>
        <data android:mimeType="application/vnd.google.panorama360+jpg"/>
        <data android:mimeType="image/*"/>
        <data android:mimeType="video/*"/>
    </intent-filter>
</activity>
```

첫 번째 액티비티인 MainActivity는 앱의 주요 진입 지점이다. 사용자가 시작 관리자 아이콘을 사용하여 앱을 처음 시작할 때 열리는 액티비티이다.

ACTION_MAIN 작업은 주요 진입 지점이며 어느 인텐트 데이터도 나타나지 않는다. CATEGORY_LAUNCHER 카테고리는 이 액티비티의 아이콘이 시스템의 앱 시작 관리자에 배치되어야 한다는 것을 나타낸다. 〈activity〉 요소가 아이콘을 icon으로 지정하지 않은 경우, 시스템은 〈application〉 요소로부터 가져온 아이콘을 사용한다. 이들 두 가지가 짝을 이루어야 액티비티가 앱 시작 관리자에 나타날 수 있다.

두 번째 액티비티인 ShareActivity는 텍스트와 미디어 콘텐츠 공유를 용이하게 할 목적으로 만들어졌다. 사용자가 MainActivity에서 이 액티비티로 이동하여 진입할 수도 있지만, 두 가지 인텐트 필터 중 하나와 일치하는 암시적 인텐트를 발생시키는 또 다른 앱에서 ShareActivity에 직접 진입할 수도 있습니다.

참고로 MIME 유형, 즉 application/vnd.google.panorama360+jpg는 파노라마 사진을 지정하는 특수 데이터 유형으로, Google Panorama API로 처리할 수 있다.

8.2 명시적 인텐트를 이용하는 예제를 만들기

이 예제에는 두 가지 타입의 명시적 인테트가 있다. 첫 번째는 인텐트 데이터를 사용하지 않고 화면전환을 하는 것이고 두 번째는 인텐트 데이터를 사용하여 화면전환을 하는 것이다.

사용할 두 가지의 Activity (Sub1, Sub2)를 만들자.

Android Studio에서 새로운 Activity를 쉽게 만드는 메뉴를 제공한다. [그림 8-2]처럼 /java/패키지/에서 마우스 오른쪽 키를 눌러 "New" -> "Activity" -> "Empty Activity"를 선택한다.

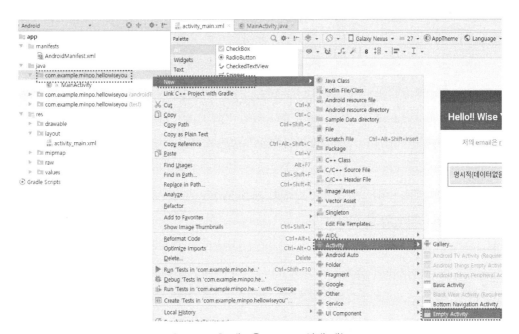

[그림 8-2] 새로운 Activity 선택 메뉴

"Empty Activity" 메뉴를 선택하면 [그림 8-3]과 같은 메뉴가 나온다. 이 메뉴에서 "Sub1 Activity"를 입력하고 "Finish" 버튼을 선택한다.

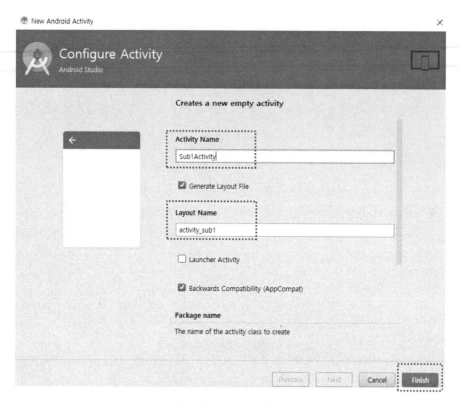

[그림 8-3] Activity 이름 설정

"Finish" 버튼 선택 후에 [그림 8-4]처럼 "Sub1Activity.java", "activity_sub1.xml" 파일이 자동 생성된 것을 확인할 수 있다.

[그림 8-4] 새로운 Activity 생성 (java, xml)

AndroidMainfest.xml 파일에도 Sub1Activity가 추가된 것을 확인할 수 있다.

```xml
<?xml version="1.0" encoding="utf-8"?>
<manifest xmlns:android="http://schemas.android.com/apk/res/android"
    package="com.example.minpo.hellowiseyou">

    <application
        android:allowBackup="true"
        android:icon="@mipmap/ic_launcher"
        android:label="@string/app_name"
        android:roundIcon="@mipmap/ic_launcher_round"
        android:supportsRtl="true"
        android:theme="@style/AppTheme">
        <activity android:name=".MainActivity">
            <intent-filter>
                <action android:name="android.intent.action.MAIN" />

                <category android:name="android.intent.category.LAUNCHER" />
            </intent-filter>
        </activity>
        <activity android:name=".Sub1Activity"> </activity>
    </application>

</manifest>
```

두 번째 Activy도 추가하자.

[그림 8-4] Activity 추가

데이터를 포함하지 않고 Sub1Activity를 호출하는 코드를 작성하자.

```
[MainActivity.java]

protected void onCreate(Bundle savedInstanceState) {
        super.onCreate(savedInstanceState);
        setContentView(R.layout.activity_main);

        Button fa = (Button) findViewById(R.id.button9);
        fa.setOnClickListener(new View.OnClickListener() {
            @Override
            public void onClick(View view) {
                Intent in = new Intent(MainActivity.this, Sub1Activity.class);
                startActivity(in);
            }
        });
}
```

[Sub1Activity.java]

```java
public class Sub1Activity extends AppCompatActivity {

    @Override
    protected void onCreate(Bundle savedInstanceState) {
        super.onCreate(savedInstanceState);
        setContentView(R.layout.activity_sub1);

        Button fin = (Button) findViewById(R.id.button11);

        fin.setOnClickListener(new View.OnClickListener() {
            @Override
            public void onClick(View view) {
                finish(); //현재 activity 닫기
            }
        });
    }
}
```

[AndroidManifest.xml]

```xml
<?xml version="1.0" encoding="utf-8"?>
<manifest xmlns:android="http://schemas.android.com/apk/res/android"
    package="com.example.minpo.hellowiseyou">

    <application
        android:allowBackup="true"
        android:icon="@mipmap/ic_launcher"
        android:label="@string/app_name"
        android:roundIcon="@mipmap/ic_launcher_round"
        android:supportsRtl="true"
        android:theme="@style/AppTheme">
        <activity android:name=".MainActivity">
            <intent-filter>
                <action android:name="android.intent.action.MAIN" />

                <category android:name="android.intent.category.LAUNCHER" />
            </intent-filter>
        </activity>
```

```
    <activity android:name=".Sub1Activity" />
      <activity android:name=".Sub2Activity"></activity>
  </application>

</manifest>
```

[실행 결과]

다음은 두 번째 Activity인 Sub2Activity를 호출한다. 이번 호출의 경우에는 화면의
EditText에 입력하는 텍스트를 Sub2Activity의 화면에 출력하자.
[MainActivity.java]에서 putExtra() 함수를 사용하여 전달할 데이터를 지정한다. 문법은
"key:value"의 개념을 "data"라는 key에 전달할 데이터를 연결한다.

[MainActivity.java]

```java
protected void onCreate(Bundle savedInstanceState) {
        super.onCreate(savedInstanceState);
        setContentView(R.layout.activity_main);

        Button fa = (Button) findViewById(R.id.button9);
        fa.setOnClickListener(new View.OnClickListener() {
            @Override
            public void onClick(View view) {
                Intent in = new Intent(MainActivity.this, Sub1Activity.class);
                startActivity(in);
            }
        });

        Button sa = (Button) findViewById(R.id.button10);
        sa.setOnClickListener(new View.OnClickListener() {
            @Override
            public void onClick(View view) {
                Intent in = new Intent(MainActivity.this, Sub2Activity.class);
                EditText et = (EditText) findViewById(R.id.editText);
                String input = et.getText().toString();
                in.putExtra("data", input);
                startActivity(in);
            }
        });
```

[Sub2Activity.java]

```java
public class Sub2Activity extends AppCompatActivity {

    @Override
    protected void onCreate(Bundle savedInstanceState) {
        super.onCreate(savedInstanceState);
        setContentView(R.layout.activity_sub2);

        Intent in = new Intent(this.getIntent());
        String receivedData = in.getStringExtra("data");
```

```
            TextView tv = (TextView) findViewById(R.id.textView3);
            tv.setText(receivedData);

            final Button finish = (Button) findViewById(R.id.button12);
            finish.setOnClickListener(new View.OnClickListener() {
                @Override
                public void onClick(View view) {
                    finish();
                }
            });


        }
}
```

[AndroidManifest.xml]
```xml
<?xml version="1.0" encoding="utf-8"?>
<manifest xmlns:android="http://schemas.android.com/apk/res/android"
    package="com.example.minpo.hellowiseyou">

    <application
        android:allowBackup="true"
        android:icon="@mipmap/ic_launcher"
        android:label="@string/app_name"
        android:roundIcon="@mipmap/ic_launcher_round"
        android:supportsRtl="true"
        android:theme="@style/AppTheme">
        <activity android:name=".MainActivity">
            <intent-filter>
                <action android:name="android.intent.action.MAIN" />

                <category android:name="android.intent.category.LAUNCHER" />
            </intent-filter>
        </activity>
        <activity android:name=".Sub1Activity" />
        <activity android:name=".Sub2Activity"></activity>
    </application>

</manifest>
```

[실행 결과]

다음은 세 번째 Activity인 Sub3Activity를 호출한다. 이번 호출의 경우에는 화면의 EditText에 입력하는 텍스트를 Sub3Activity의 화면에 출력하고 입력된 문자열의 길이를 구한다. 문자열의 길이를 호출한 MainActivity로 되돌려 주는 기능을 구현한다.

이 기능을 구현하기 위해, [MainActivity.java]에서 putExtra() 함수를 사용하여 전달할 데 이터를 지정한다. startActivity() 함수 대신에 startActivityForResult() 함수를 사용한다. Sub3Activity에서 문자열의 길이를 되돌려 받기 위해 onActivityResult() 함수를 구현해야 한다.

```java
[MainActivity.java]

protected void onCreate(Bundle savedInstanceState) {
        super.onCreate(savedInstanceState);
        setContentView(R.layout.activity_main);

        Button returnvaelue = (Button) findViewById(R.id.button14);
        returnvaelue.setOnClickListener(new View.OnClickListener() {
            @Override
            public void onClick(View view) {
                Intent in = new Intent(MainActivity.this, Sub3Activity.class);
                EditText et = (EditText) findViewById(R.id.editText);
                String input = et.getText().toString();
                in.putExtra("data", input);
                startActivityForResult(in, 9999); //9999:임의로 정한 수
            }
        });
}


protected void onActivityResult(int requestCode, int resultcode, Intent data)
{
        switch(requestCode) {
            case 9999 :
                if(resultcode == RESULT_OK) {
                    EditText et = (EditText) findViewById(R.id.editText);
                    String resultData = data.getStringExtra("LENGTH");
                    et.setText(resultData);
                }
        }
}

[Sub3Activity.java]

public class Sub3Activity extends AppCompatActivity {

    @Override
    protected void onCreate(Bundle savedInstanceState) {
        super.onCreate(savedInstanceState);
        setContentView(R.layout.activity_sub3);
```

```java
Intent in = new Intent(this.getIntent());
String receivedData = in.getStringExtra("data");

TextView tv = (TextView) findViewById(R.id.textView6);
tv.setText(receivedData.length() + " 길이 입니다.");

Intent out = new Intent();
out.putExtra("LENGTH", receivedData.length()+"");
setResult(RESULT_OK, out);

Button finish = (Button) findViewById(R.id.button13);
finish.setOnClickListener(new View.OnClickListener() {
    @Override
    public void onClick(View view) {
        finish();
    }
});
    }
}
```

[AndroidManifest.xml]

```xml
<?xml version="1.0" encoding="utf-8"?>
<manifest xmlns:android="http://schemas.android.com/apk/res/android"
    package="com.example.minpo.hellowiseyou">

    <application
        android:allowBackup="true"
        android:icon="@mipmap/ic_launcher"
        android:label="@string/app_name"
        android:roundIcon="@mipmap/ic_launcher_round"
        android:supportsRtl="true"
        android:theme="@style/AppTheme">
        <activity android:name=".MainActivity">
            <intent-filter>
                <action android:name="android.intent.action.MAIN" />

                <category android:name="android.intent.category.LAUNCHER" />
            </intent-filter>
```

```
        </activity>
        <activity android:name=".Sub1Activity" />
        <activity android:name=".Sub2Activity" />
        <activity android:name=".Sub3Activity"></activity>
    </application>

</manifest>
```

[실행 결과]

[1]   Android Intent 및 Intent Filter, https://developer.android.com/guide/topics/manifest/action-element.html

[2]   Android Action, https://developer.android.com/guide/topics/manifest/action-element.html

안드로이드 데이터베이스의 이해와 응용

이번 장에서는 사용자 데이터를 영구히 보존하는 방법을 살펴본다. 일반적으로 SharedPreferences를 사용하여 설정 정보와 같은 간단한 데이터를 저장하는 방법, 파일을 직접 생성하여 입출력하는 방법, SQL을 이용하여 로컬 데이터베이스에 저장하는 방법 등이 있다. 9장에서는 SQL을 이용하여 로컬 데이터베이스에 저장하고 검색하는 방법을 살펴본다.

9.1 SQLite를 이해하기

학습목표

데이터베이스의 정의와 안드로이드 폰에서 데이터베이스를 사용하는 방법을 이해한다.

SQLite[1]는 MySQL이나 PostgreSQL과 같은 데이터베이스관리 시스팀(DBMS)이지만, 서버가 아니라 으용 프로그램에 넣어 사용하는 비교적 가벼운 데이터베이스이다[2]. 영어권에서는 "에스큐엘라이트" 또는 "시퀄라이트"라고 읽는다.

일반적인 RDBMS에 비해 대규모 작업에는 적합하지 않지만, 중소 규모라면 속도에 손색이 없다. 또 API는 단순히 라이브러리를 호출하는 것만 있으며, 데이터를 저장하는 데 하나의 파일만을 사용하는 것이 특징이다. 버전 3.3.8에서는 풀텍스트 검색 기능을 가진 FTS1 모듈이 지원된다. 컬럼을 삭제하거나 변경하는 것 등이 제한된다.

구글 안드로이드 운영 체제에 기본 탑재된 데이터베이스이기도 하다. 안드로이드 디바이스에서 SQLite를 사용하기 위해 단순히 API 함수만 호출하면 데이터베이스를 위한 기능을 사용할 수 있다. 특히, 모든 데이터는 하나의 파일에 저장된다.

SQLite는 관계형 데이터베이스이며 이를 사용하기 위해 테이블(Table)이 기본 단위가 된다. 테이블은 컬럼(Column)과 로우(Row)로 구성된다.

관계형 데이터베이스 내의 데이터를 다루기 위해 SQL(Structured Query Language)라는 표준 언어를 사용한다. SQL로 데이터베이스 스키마 생성 및 수정, 테이블 수정, 삭제, 추가, 조회 등의 기본 작업을 수행할 수 있다.

SQL에 정의된 명령어는 데이터 정의 언어(DDL, Data Definition Language), 데이터 처리 언어(DML, Data Manipulation Language), 데이터 제어 언어(DCL, Data Control Language) 가 있다.

데이터 정의 언어는 CREATE, ALTER, DROP 명령어로 구성되며 데이터베이스 자체를 만들고 변경하고 삭제한다.

데이터 조작어는 INSERT, UPDATE, DELETE, SELECT 명령어 구성되며 테이블에 데이터를 추가, 갱신, 삭제, 조회한다.

데이터 제어 언어는 GRANT, BEGIN, COMMIT, ROLLBACK 명령어로 구성되고 권한 설정, 트랜잭션 시작, 트랜잭션 결과 적용, 트랜잭션 취소한다.

9.2 안드로이드에서 SQLite를 사용해보기

안드로이드에서 SQLite를 사용하기 위해 "android.data.sqlite" 패키지[3]를 사용한다. SQLite 데이터베이스에 데이터를 추가, 삭제, 수정, 조회하기 위해 SQLiteDatabase 클래스[4]를 사용한다.

SQLiteDatabase

```
public final class SQLiteDatabase
extends SQLiteClosable
```

java.lang.Object
        ∟ android.database.sqlite.SQLiteClosable
                ∟ android.database.sqlite.SQLiteDatabase

[그림 9-1] SQLiteDatabase 클래스 상속도

먼저, SQLite 데이터베이스 사용하기 위해 우선적으로 해야 하는 일이 데이터베이스 파일을 열거나 만들어야 한다. 이를 위해 SQLiteDatabase 클래스에서 정의된 "openDatabase()", "openOrCreateDatabase()"를 사용한다. 데이터베이스가 이미 존재하는 경우는 "openDatabase()"를 사용하고 데이터베이스가 없을 수도 있다면 "openOrCreateDatabase()" 함수를 사용한다.

다음의 예는 "openOrCreateDatabase()" 함수를 사용하여 "ysucomputer.db"가 존재하지 않는다면 생성후에 데이터베이스를 열게 되는 예제이다. 만약 데이터베이스를 생성하거나 열수 없다면 "SQLiteExcpeiton" 예외(Exception)이 발생한다.

```
protected void onCreate(Bundle savedInstanceState) {
        super.onCreate(savedInstanceState);
        setContentView(R.layout.activity_main);

        SQLiteDatabase sqLiteDatabase = null;

        try {
            sqLiteDatabase = SQLiteDatabase.openOrCreateDatabase("ysucomputer.db",
null);
        } catch (SQLiteAbortException e) {
            e.printStackTrace();
        }
}
```

위의 코드를 안드로이드 디바이스에서 실행하면 "java.lang.RuntimeException: Unable to start activity ComponentInfo{com.example.minpo.hellowiseyou/ com.example. minpo.hellowiseyou.MainActivity}: android.database.sqlite. SQLiteCantOpen DatabaseException: unknown error (code 14): Could not open database"라는 오류가 발생할 수 있다. 이 오류의 원인을 살펴보면 /data/data/0/com.example.minpo. hellowiseyou/databases/ysucomputer.db 파일이 생성할 수 없기 때문에 발생한다.

이 오류를 다음과 같이 수정한다.

```
protected void onCreate(Bundle savedInstanceState) {
        super.onCreate(savedInstanceState);
        setContentView(R.layout.activity_main);

        SQLiteDatabase sqLiteDatabase = null;
        String dbFile = "ysucomputer.db";
```

```
        try {
            File databasefile = getDatabasePath(dbFile);
            sqLiteDatabase = SQLiteDatabase.openOrCreateDatabase(databasefile, null);
        } catch (Exception e) {
            String databasePath = getFilesDir().getPath() + "/" + dbFile;
            File databasefile = new File(databasePath);
            sqLiteDatabase = SQLiteDatabase.openOrCreateDatabase(databasefile, null);
        }
    }
```

다음 단계는 SQLite 데이터베이스 파일을 열 수 있다면 SQLiteDatabase 객체의 참조
(reference)를 얻을 수 있다. 이 참조를 이용하여 데이터베이스에 데이터를 추가, 삭제, 조
회를 할 수 있다. 데이터베이스의 참조를 얻었다고 해서 바로 데이터를 추가할 수 없다.
아직 관계형 데이터베이스의 테이블이 아직 만들어지지 않았다. 이 테이블은 데이터의
속성과 값의 관계를 표현한다. 아직 만들어지지 않은 테이블을 만들어보자.

```
protected void onCreate(Bundle savedInstanceState) {
        super.onCreate(savedInstanceState);
        setContentView(R.layout.activity_main);

        SQLiteDatabase sqLiteDatabase = null;
        String dbFile = "ysucomputer.db";

        try {
            File databasefile = getDatabasePath(dbFile);
            sqLiteDatabase = SQLiteDatabase.openOrCreateDatabase(databasefile,
null);
        } catch (Exception e) {
            String databasePath = getFilesDir().getPath() + "/" + dbFile;
            File databasefile = new File(databasePath);
            sqLiteDatabase = SQLiteDatabase.openOrCreateDatabase(databasefile,
null);
        }
    }
```

테이블이 안드로이드 앱이 실행될 때마다 만들어지면 안 되기 때문에, 아래와 같이 "If not exit"라는 조건을 넣게 된다.

"Create tabel"에서 사용될 수 있는 데이터 타입[5]은 다음과 같다.

데이터 타입	사용할 수 있는 데이터
text, varchar	문자열
smallint, integer	정수(2 바이트, 4바이트)
real, float, double	소수(4바이트, 8바이트)
boolean	true, false
date,time,timestamp	시간
blob,binary	바이너리

아래의 코드에서 테이블을 생성하는 코드를 보여준다. 테이블명은 order_t이고 정수 (integer) 타입의 no 변수와 text 타입의 name 변수를 선언한다.

```java
Button dbTableCreate = (Button) findViewById(R.id.button16);
        dbTableCreate.setOnClickListener(new View.OnClickListener() {
          @Override
          public void onClick(View view) {
              String sqlCreateTable = "Create table if not exists order_t(no
integer, name text)";
              sqLiteDatabase.execSQL(sqlCreateTable);
          }
        });
}
```

다음 단계는 SQL 명령어인 INSERT를 사용하여 데이터를 삽입하는 방법을 볼 수 있다. 앞의 테이블 구조에서 정의한대로, 나이를 저장하는 no 변수, 이름을 저장하는 name 변수를 사용한다.

```
Button insertData = (Button) findViewById(R.id.button17);
        insertData.setOnClickListener(new View.OnClickListener() {
            @Override
            public void onClick(View view) {
                String sqlInsert = "Insert into order_t(no, name) values (47,
'minpo jung')";
                sqLiteDatabase.execSQL(sqlInsert);
            }
        });
    }
```

다음 단계는 SQL 조회 명령어인 "select"를 사용하여 입력된 데이터를 조회하는 기능이다. "select * from order_t"는 order_t 테이블에 있는 모든 데이터를 조회하라는 의미이다. 조회된 데이터는 조회된 데이터의 위치 정보를 나타내는 "커서(Cursor)"를 이용하여 데이터를 찾아간다. 첫 번째 칼럼은 정수 타입의 나이를 의미하고 두 번째 칼럼은 문자열 타입의 이름을 의미한다. 데이터베이스에서 찾은 데이터를 텍스트뷰에 보여준다.

```
Button selectData = (Button) findViewById(R.id.button18);
        selectData.setOnClickListener(new View.OnClickListener() {
            @Override
            public void onClick(View view) {
                TextView t = (TextView) findViewById(R.id.textView10);
                String sqlSelect = "select * from order_t";
                Cursor c = null;
                c = sqLiteDatabase.rawQuery(sqlSelect, null);
                while(c.moveToNext()) {
                    int old = c.getInt(0);
                    String name = c.getString(1);
                    t.setText("old: " + old + ", name: " + name);
                }

            }
        });
    }
```

다음 단계는 SQL 명령어 UPDATE를 사용하여 입력된 데이터 중에 특정 조건을 만족하는 데이터의 값을 수정한다. 예제에서는 이름이 'minpo jung'인 데이터를 찾아 나이를 50으로 변경한다.

```
Button updateData = (Button) findViewById(R.id.button);
    updateData.setOnClickListener(new View.OnClickListener() {
        @Override
        public void onClick(View view) {
            String sqlUpdate = "update order_t set no=50, name='minpo
jung' where name='minpo jung'";
            sqLiteDatabase.execSQL(sqlUpdate);
        }
    });
```

다음 단계는 SQL 명령어 DELETE를 사용하여 데이터를 포함하고 있는 테이블(Table)의 데이터를 모두 삭제한다. 이 명령어는 모든 데이터를 삭제하니 주의하여 사용해야 한다.

```
Button deleteTable = (Button) findViewById(R.id.button2);
    deleteTable.setOnClickListener(new View.OnClickListener() {
        @Override
        public void onClick(View view) {
            String sqlDelete = "Delete from order_t";
            sqLiteDatabase.execSQL(sqlDelete);
        }
    });
```

다음 단계는 SQL 명령어 DROP을 사용하여 테이블(Table) 자체를 삭제한다. 이 명령어는 데이터뿐만 아니라 데이터의 구조를 표현하는 테이블까지 삭제하기 때문에 주의하여 사용해야 한다.

```
Button dropTable = (Button) findViewById(R.id.button3);
        dropTable.setOnClickListener(new View.OnClickListener() {
            @Override
            public void onClick(View view) {
                String sqlDrop = "Drop table order_t";
                sqLiteDatabase.execSQL(sqlDrop);
            }
        });
```

이제 앞에서 설명한 모든 코드를 이용하여 예제를 작성하자.

```
public class MainActivity extends AppCompatActivity {
    SQLiteDatabase sqLiteDatabase = null;
    String dbFile = "ysucomputer.db";

    @Override
    protected void onCreate(Bundle savedInstanceState) {
        super.onCreate(savedInstanceState);
        setContentView(R.layout.activity_main);

        Button dbCreate = (Button) findViewById(R.id.button15);
        dbCreate.setOnClickListener(new View.OnClickListener() {
            @Override
            public void onClick(View view) {
                try {
                    File databasefile = getDatabasePath(dbFile);
                    sqLiteDatabase                                             =
SQLiteDatabase.openOrCreateDatabase(databasefile,  null);
                } catch (Exception e) {
                    String databasePath = getFilesDir().getPath() + "/" + dbFile;
                    File databasefile = new File(databasePath);
                    sqLiteDatabase = SQLiteDatabase.openOrCreateDatabase(databasefile,
null);
                }
            }
        });
```

```java
        Button dbTableCreate = (Button) findViewById(R.id.button16);
        dbTableCreate.setOnClickListener(new View.OnClickListener() {
            @Override
            public void onClick(View view) {
                String sqlCreateTable = "Create table if not exists order_t(no
integer, name text)";
                sqLiteDatabase.execSQL(sqlCreateTable);
            }
        });


        Button insertData = (Button) findViewById(R.id.button17);
        insertData.setOnClickListener(new View.OnClickListener() {
            @Override
            public void onClick(View view) {
                String sqlInsert = "Insert into order_t(no, name) values (47,
'minpo jung')";
                sqLiteDatabase.execSQL(sqlInsert);
            }
        });


        Button selectData = (Button) findViewById(R.id.button18);
        selectData.setOnClickListener(new View.OnClickListener() {
            @Override
            public void onClick(View view) {
                TextView t = (TextView) findViewById(R.id.textView10);
                String sqlSelect = "select * from order_t";
                Cursor c = null;
                c = sqLiteDatabase.rawQuery(sqlSelect, null);
                while(c.moveToNext()) {
                    int old = c.getInt(0);
                    String name = c.getString(1);
                    t.setText("old: " + old + ", name: " + name);
                }

            }
        });
```

```
        Button updateData = (Button) findViewById(R.id.button);
        updateData.setOnClickListener(new View.OnClickListener() {
            @Override
            public void onClick(View view) {
                String sqlUpdate = "update order_t set no=50, name='minpo
jung' where name='minpo jung'";
                sqLiteDatabase.execSQL(sqlUpdate);
            }
        });

        Button deleteData = (Button) findViewById(R.id.button2);
        deleteData.setOnClickListener(new View.OnClickListener() {
            @Override
            public void onClick(View view) {
                String sqlDelete = "Delete from order_t";
                sqLiteDatabase.execSQL(sqlDelete);
            }
        });

        Button dropTable = (Button) findViewById(R.id.button3);
        dropTable.setOnClickListener(new View.OnClickListener() {
            @Override
            public void onClick(View view) {
                String sqlDrop = "Drop table order_t";
                sqLiteDatabase.execSQL(sqlDrop);
            }
        });
    }
}
```

[실행 결과]

앱을 처음 실행하면 (1) 데이터베이스만들기, (2) 테이블 만들기, (3) 테이블 데이터 모두 삭제하기, (4) 테이블에 데이터 추가하기, (5) 테이블 삭제하기, (6) 조회하기, (7) 업데이트 버튼이 나타난다.

처음에 (1)번 버튼은 항상 눌러야 한다. 데이터베이스가 있다면 생성하지 않고, 없다면 데이터베이스를 생성한다.

(2)번 버튼을 눌러 데이터의 구조를 정의하는 테이블을 생성한다. 같은 이름의 테이블이 있다면 생성하지 않는다.

(4)번 버튼을 눌러 생성된 테이블에 데이터를 추가한다. 누를 때마다 데이터가 추가된다.

(6)번 버튼을 눌러 현재 입력된 데이터를 TextView에서 확인할 수 있다.

(7)번 버튼을 눌러 현재 입력된 데이터를 업데이트 할 수 있다.

(3)번 버튼을 눌러 입력된 모든 데이터를 삭제할 수 있다.

(5)번 버튼을 눌러 생성된 테이블을 없앨 수 있다.

참·고·자·료

[1]   SQLite 정보, http://www.sqlite.org

[2]   SQLite 위키정보, https://ko.wikipedia.org/wiki/SQLite

[3]   android.data.sqlite 패키지 정보, https://developer.android.com/reference/
       android/database/sqlite/package-summary.html?hl=ko

[4]   SQLiteDatabase 클래스 정보, https://developer.android.com/reference/android/
       database/sqlite/SQLiteDatabase.html

부록

[부록 A] AudioManger Class SDK 설명서

(https://developer.android.com/reference/android/media/AudioManager.html)

Nested classes	
class	AudioManager.AudioPlaybackCallback Interface for receiving update notifications about the playback activity on the system.
class	AudioManager.AudioRecordingCallback Interface for receiving update notifications about the recording configuration.
interface	AudioManager.OnAudioFocusChangeListener Interface definition for a callback to be invoked when the audio focus of the system is updated.

Constants	
String	ACTION_AUDIO_BECOMING_NOISY Broadcast intent, a hint for applications that audio is about to become 'noisy' due to a change in audio outputs.
String	ACTION_HDMI_AUDIO_PLUG Broadcast Action: A sticky broadcast indicating an HDMI cable was plugged or unplugged.
String	ACTION_HEADSET_PLUG Broadcast Action: Wired Headset plugged in or unplugged.
String	ACTION_SCO_AUDIO_STATE_CHANGED *This constant was deprecated in API level 14. Use ACTION_SCO_AUDIO_STATE_UPDATED instead*
String	ACTION_SCO_AUDIO_STATE_UPDATED Sticky broadcast intent action indicating that the bluetoooth SCO audio connection state has been updated.
int	ADJUST_LOWER Decrease the ringer volume.
int	ADJUST_MUTE Mute the volume.
int	ADJUST_RAISE Increase the ringer volume.

int	ADJUST_SAME Maintain the previous ringer volume.
int	ADJUST_TOGGLE_MUTE Toggle the mute state.
int	ADJUST_UNMUTE Unmute the volume.
int	AUDIOFOCUS_GAIN Used to indicate a gain of audio focus, or a request of audio focus, of unknown duration.
int	AUDIOFOCUS_GAIN_TRANSIENT Used to indicate a temporary gain or request of audio focus, anticipated to last a short amount of time.
int	AUDIOFOCUS_GAIN_TRANSIENT_EXCLUSIVE Used to indicate a temporary request of audio focus, anticipated to last a short amount of time, during which no other applications, or system components, should play anything.
int	AUDIOFOCUS_GAIN_TRANSIENT_MAY_DUCK Used to indicate a temporary request of audio focus, anticipated to last a short amount of time, and where it is acceptable for other audio applications to keep playing after having lowered their output level (also referred to as "ducking").
int	AUDIOFOCUS_LOSS Used to indicate a loss of audio focus of unknown duration.
int	AUDIOFOCUS_LOSS_TRANSIENT Used to indicate a transient loss of audio focus.
int	AUDIOFOCUS_LOSS_TRANSIENT_CAN_DUCK Used to indicate a transient loss of audio focus where the loser of the audio focus can lower its output volume if it wants to continue playing (also referred to as "ducking"), as the new focus owner doesn't require others to be silent.
int	AUDIOFOCUS_NONE Used to indicate no audio focus has been gained or lost, or requested.
int	AUDIOFOCUS_REQUEST_DELAYED A focus change request whose granting is delayed: the request was successful, but the requester will only be granted audio focus once the condition that prevented immediate granting has ended.
int	AUDIOFOCUS_REQUEST_FAILED A failed focus change request.

int	AUDIOFOCUS_REQUEST_GRANTED A successful focus change request.
int	AUDIO_SESSION_ID_GENERATE A special audio session ID to indicate that the audio session ID isn't known and the framework should generate a new value.
int	ERROR A default error code.
int	ERROR_DEAD_OBJECT An error code indicating that the object reporting it is no longer valid and needs to be recreated.
String	EXTRA_AUDIO_PLUG_STATE Extra used in ACTION_HDMI_AUDIO_PLUG to communicate whether HDMI is plugged in or unplugged.
String	EXTRA_ENCODINGS Extra used in ACTION_HDMI_AUDIO_PLUG to define the audio encodings supported by the connected HDMI device.
String	EXTRA_MAX_CHANNEL_COUNT Extra used in ACTION_HDMI_AUDIO_PLUG to define the maximum number of channels supported by the HDMI device.
String	EXTRA_RINGER_MODE The new ringer mode.
String	EXTRA_SCO_AUDIO_PREVIOUS_STATE Extra for intent ACTION_SCO_AUDIO_STATE_UPDATED containing the previous bluetooth SCO connection state.
String	EXTRA_SCO_AUDIO_STATE Extra for intent ACTION_SCO_AUDIO_STATE_CHANGED or ACTION_SCO_AUDIO_STATE_UPDATED containing the new bluetooth SCO connection state.
String	EXTRA_VIBRATE_SETTING *This constant was deprecated in API level 16. Applications should maintain their own vibrate policy based on current ringer mode and listen to RINGER_MODE_CHANGED_ACTION instead.*
String	EXTRA_VIBRATE_TYPE *This constant was deprecated in API level 16. Applications should maintain their own vibrate policy based on current ringer mode and listen to RINGER_MODE_CHANGED_ACTION instead.*
int	FLAG_ALLOW_RINGER_MODES Whether to include ringer modes as possible options when changing volume.

int	FLAG_PLAY_SOUND Whether to play a sound when changing the volume.
int	FLAG_REMOVE_SOUND_AND_VIBRATE Removes any sounds/vibrate that may be in the queue, or are playing (related to changing volume).
int	FLAG_SHOW_UI Show a toast containing the current volume.
int	FLAG_VIBRATE Whether to vibrate if going into the vibrate ringer mode.
int	FX_FOCUS_NAVIGATION_DOWN Focus has moved down
int	FX_FOCUS_NAVIGATION_LEFT Focus has moved left
int	FX_FOCUS_NAVIGATION_RIGHT Focus has moved right
int	FX_FOCUS_NAVIGATION_UP Focus has moved up
int	FX_KEYPRESS_DELETE IME delete keypress sound
int	FX_KEYPRESS_INVALID Invalid keypress sound
int	FX_KEYPRESS_RETURN IME return_keypress sound
int	FX_KEYPRESS_SPACEBAR IME spacebar keypress sound
int	FX_KEYPRESS_STANDARD IME standard keypress sound
int	FX_KEY_CLICK Keyboard and direction pad click sound
int	GET_DEVICES_ALL Specifies to the getDevices(int) method to include both source and sink devices.
int	GET_DEVICES_INPUTS Specifies to the getDevices(int) method to include source (i.e.
int	GET_DEVICES_OUTPUTS Specifies to the getDevices(int) method to include sink (i.e.
int	MODE_CURRENT Current audio mode.

int	MODE_INVALID Invalid audio mode.
int	MODE_IN_CALL In call audio mode.
int	MODE_IN_COMMUNICATION In communication audio mode.
int	MODE_NORMAL Normal audio mode: not ringing and no call established.
int	MODE_RINGTONE Ringing audio mode.
int	NUM_STREAMS *This constant was deprecated in API level 3. Do not iterate on volume stream type values.*
String	PROPERTY_OUTPUT_FRAMES_PER_BUFFER Used as a key for getProperty(String) to request the native or optimal output buffer size for this device's low latency output stream, in decimal PCM frames.
String	PROPERTY_OUTPUT_SAMPLE_RATE Used as a key for getProperty(String) to request the native or optimal output sample rate for this device's low latency output stream, in decimal Hz.
String	PROPERTY_SUPPORT_AUDIO_SOURCE_UNPROCESSED Used as a key for getProperty(String) to determine if the unprocessed audio source is available and supported with the expected frequency range and level response.
String	PROPERTY_SUPPORT_MIC_NEAR_ULTRASOUND Used as a key for getProperty(String) to determine if the default microphone audio source supports near-ultrasound frequencies (range of 18 – 21 kHz).
String	PROPERTY_SUPPORT_SPEAKER_NEAR_ULTRASOUND Used as a key for getProperty(String) to determine if the default speaker audio path supports near-ultrasound frequencies (range of 18 – 21 kHz).
String	RINGER_MODE_CHANGED_ACTION Sticky broadcast intent action indicating that the ringer mode has changed.
int	RINGER_MODE_NORMAL Ringer mode that may be audible and may vibrate.

int	RINGER_MODE_SILENT Ringer mode that will be silent and will not vibrate.
int	RINGER_MODE_VIBRATE Ringer mode that will be silent and will vibrate.
int	ROUTE_ALL *This constant was deprecated in API level 5. Do not set audio routing directly, use setSpeakerphoneOn(), setBluetoothScoOn() methods instead.*
int	ROUTE_BLUETOOTH *This constant was deprecated in API level 3. use ROUTE_BLUETOOTH_SCODo not set audio routing directly, use setSpeakerphoneOn(), setBluetoothScoOn() methods instead.*
int	ROUTE_BLUETOOTH_A2DP *This constant was deprecated in API level 5. Do not set audio routing directly, use setSpeakerphoneOn(), setBluetoothScoOn() methods instead.*
int	ROUTE_BLUETOOTH_SCO *This constant was deprecated in API level 5. Do not set audio routing directly, use setSpeakerphoneOn(), setBluetoothScoOn() methods instead.*
int	ROUTE_EARPIECE *This constant was deprecated in API level 5. Do not set audio routing directly, use setSpeakerphoneOn(), setBluetoothScoOn() methods instead.*
int	ROUTE_HEADSET *This constant was deprecated in API level 5. Do not set audio routing directly, use setSpeakerphoneOn(), setBluetoothScoOn() methods instead.*
int	ROUTE_SPEAKER *This constant was deprecated in API level 5. Do not set audio routing directly, use setSpeakerphoneOn(), setBluetoothScoOn() methods instead.*
int	SCO_AUDIO_STATE_CONNECTED Value for extra EXTRA_SCO_AUDIO_STATE or EXTRA_SCO_AUDIO_PREVIOUS_STATE indicating that the SCO audio channel is established
int	SCO_AUDIO_STATE_CONNECTING Value for extra EXTRA_SCO_AUDIO_STATE or EXTRA_SCO_AUDIO_PREVIOUS_STATE indicating that the SCO audio channel is being established

int	SCO_AUDIO_STATE_DISCONNECTED Value for extra EXTRA_SCO_AUDIO_STATE or EXTRA_SCO_AUDIO_PREVIOUS_STATE indicating that the SCO audio channel is not established
int	SCO_AUDIO_STATE_ERROR Value for extra EXTRA_SCO_AUDIO_STATE indicating that there was an error trying to obtain the state
int	STREAM_ACCESSIBILITY Used to identify the volume of audio streams for accessibility prompts
int	STREAM_ALARM Used to identify the volume of audio streams for alarms
int	STREAM_DTMF Used to identify the volume of audio streams for DTMF Tones
int	STREAM_MUSIC Used to identify the volume of audio streams for music playback
int	STREAM_NOTIFICATION Used to identify the volume of audio streams for notifications
int	STREAM_RING Used to identify the volume of audio streams for the phone ring
int	STREAM_SYSTEM Used to identify the volume of audio streams for system sounds
int	STREAM_VOICE_CALL Used to identify the volume of audio streams for phone calls
int	USE_DEFAULT_STREAM_TYPE Suggests using the default stream type.
String	VIBRATE_SETTING_CHANGED_ACTION *This constant was deprecated in API level 16. Applications should maintain their own vibrate policy based on current ringer mode and listen to RINGER_MODE_CHANGED_ACTION instead.*
int	VIBRATE_SETTING_OFF *This constant was deprecated in API level 16. Applications should maintain their own vibrate policy based on current ringer mode that can be queried via getRingerMode().*
int	VIBRATE_SETTING_ON *This constant was deprecated in API level 16. Applications should maintain their own vibrate policy based on current ringer mode that can be queried via getRingerMode().*

int	VIBRATE_SETTING_ONLY_SILENT *This constant was deprecated in API level 16. Applications should maintain their own vibrate policy based on current ringer mode that can be queried via getRingerMode().*
int	VIBRATE_TYPE_NOTIFICATION *This constant was deprecated in API level 16. Applications should maintain their own vibrate policy based on current ringer mode that can be queried via getRingerMode().*
int	VIBRATE_TYPE_RINGER *This constant was deprecated in API level 16. Applications should maintain their own vibrate policy based on current ringer mode that can be queried via getRingerMode().*

[부록 B] Button Class SDK 설명서

(https://developer.android.com/guide/topics/ui/controls/button.html)

TextView에서 상속받은 XML attributes

android:autoLink	Controls whether links such as urls and email addresses are automatically found and converted to clickable links.
android:autoSizeMaxTextSize	The maximum text size constraint to be used when auto-sizing text.
android:autoSizeMinTextSize	The minimum text size constraint to be used when auto-sizing text.
android:autoSizePresetSizes	Resource array of dimensions to be used in conjunction with autoSizeTextType set to uniform.
android:autoSizeStepGranularity	Specify the auto-size step size if autoSizeTextType is set to uniform.
android:autoSizeTextType	Specify the type of auto-size.
android:autoText	If set, specifies that this TextView has a textual input method and automatically corrects some common spelling errors.
android:breakStrategy	Break strategy (control over paragraph layout).
android:bufferType	Determines the minimum type that getText() will return.
android:capitalize	If set, specifies that this TextView has a textual input method and should automatically capitalize what the user types.
android:cursorVisible	Makes the cursor visible (the default) or invisible.
android:digits	If set, specifies that this TextView has a numeric input method and that these specific characters are the ones that it will accept.
android:drawableBottom	The drawable to be drawn below the text.
android:drawableEnd	The drawable to be drawn to the end of the text.
android:drawableLeft	The drawable to be drawn to the left of the text.
android:drawablePadding	The padding between the drawables and the text.
android:drawableRight	The drawable to be drawn to the right of the text.

android:drawableStart	The drawable to be drawn to the start of the text.
android:drawableTint	Tint to apply to the compound (left, top, etc.) drawables.
android:drawableTint Mode	Blending mode used to apply the compound (left, top, etc.) drawables tint.
android:drawableTop	The drawable to be drawn above the text.
android:editable	If set, specifies that this TextView has an input method.
android:editorExtras	Reference to an <input-extras> XML resource containing additional data to supply to an input method, which is private to the implementation of the input method.
android:elegantTextHeight	Elegant text height, especially for less compacted complex script text.
android:ellipsize	If set, causes words that are longer than the view is wide to be ellipsized instead of broken in the middle.
android:ems	Makes the TextView be exactly this many ems wide.
android:fontFamily	Font family (named by string) for the text.
android:fontFeatureSettings	Font feature settings.
android:freezesText	If set, the text view will include its current complete text inside of its frozen icicle in addition to meta-data such as the current cursor position.
android:gravity	Specifies how to align the text by the view's x- and/or y-axis when the text is smaller than the view.
android:height	Makes the TextView be exactly this tall.
android:hint	Hint text to display when the text is empty.
android:hyphenationFrequency	Frequency of automatic hyphenation.
android:imeActionId	Supply a value for EditorInfo.actionId used when an input method is connected to the text view.
android:imeActionLabel	Supply a value for EditorInfo.actionLabel used when an input method is connected to the text view.
android:imeOptions	Additional features you can enable in an IME associated with an editor to improve the integration with your application.
android:includeFontPadding	Leave enough room for ascenders and descenders instead of using the font ascent and descent strictly.
android:inputMethod	If set, specifies that this TextView should use the specified input method (specified by fully-qualified class name).
android:inputType	The type of data being placed in a text field, used to help an input method decide how to let the user enter text.

android:letterSpacing	Text letter-spacing.
android:lineSpacing Extra	Extra spacing between lines of text.
android:lineSpacing Multiplier	Extra spacing between lines of text, as a multiplier.
android:lines	Makes the TextView be exactly this many lines tall.
android:linksClickable	If set to false, keeps the movement method from being set to the link movement method even if autoLink causes links to be found.
android:marqueeRepe atLimit	The number of times to repeat the marquee animation.
android:maxEms	Makes the TextView be at most this many ems wide.
android:maxHeight	Makes the TextView be at most this many pixels tall.
android:maxLength	Set an input filter to constrain the text length to the specified number.
android:maxLines	Makes the TextView be at most this many lines tall.
android:maxWidth	Makes the TextView be at most this many pixels wide.
android:minEms	Makes the TextView be at least this many ems wide.
android:minHeight	Makes the TextView be at least this many pixels tall.
android:minLines	Makes the TextView be at least this many lines tall.
android:minWidth	Makes the TextView be at least this many pixels wide.
android:numeric	If set, specifies that this TextView has a numeric input method.
android:password	Whether the characters of the field are displayed as password dots instead of themselves.
android:phoneNumber	If set, specifies that this TextView has a phone number input method.
android:privateIme Options	An addition content type description to supply to the input method attached to the text view, which is private to the implementation of the input method.
android:scrollHorizont ally	Whether the text is allowed to be wider than the view (and therefore can be scrolled horizontally).
android:selectAllOnFo cus	If the text is selectable, select it all when the view takes focus.
android:shadowColor	Place a blurred shadow of text underneath the text, drawn with the specified color.
android:shadowDx	Horizontal offset of the text shadow.

android:shadowDy	Vertical offset of the text shadow.
android:shadowRadius	Blur radius of the text shadow.
android:singleLine	Constrains the text to a single horizontally scrolling line instead of letting it wrap onto multiple lines, and advances focus instead of inserting a newline when you press the enter key.
android:text	Text to display.
android:textAllCaps	Present the text in ALL CAPS.
android:textAppearance	Base text color, typeface, size, and style.
android:textColor	Text color.
android:textColorHighlight	Color of the text selection highlight.
android:textColorHint	Color of the hint text.
android:textColorLink	Text color for links.
android:textIsSelectable	Indicates that the content of a non-editable text can be selected.
android:textScaleX	Sets the horizontal scaling factor for the text.
android:textSize	Size of the text.
android:textStyle	Style (bold, italic, bolditalic) for the text.
android:typeface	Typeface (normal, sans, serif, monospace) for the text.
android:width	Makes the TextView be exactly this wide.

TextView에서 상속받은 Methods

void	addExtraDataToAccessibilityNodeInfo(AccessibilityNodeInfo info, String extraDataKey, Bundle arguments) Adds extra data to an AccessibilityNodeInfo based on an explicit request for the additional data.
void	addTextChangedListener(TextWatcher watcher) Adds a TextWatcher to the list of those whose methods are called whenever this TextView's text changes.
final void	append(CharSequence text) Convenience method to append the specified text to the TextView's display buffer, upgrading it to EDITABLE if it was not already editable.
void	append(CharSequence text, int start, int end) Convenience method to append the specified text slice to the TextView's display buffer, upgrading it to EDITABLE if it was not already editable.
void	autofill(AutofillValue value) Automatically fills the content of this view with the value.
void	beginBatchEdit()
boolean	bringPointIntoView(int offset) Move the point, specified by the offset, into the view if it is needed.
void	cancelLongPress() Cancels a pending long press.
void	clearComposingText() Use BaseInputConnection.removeComposingSpans() to remove any IME composing state from this text view.
int	computeHorizontalScrollRange() Compute the horizontal range that the horizontal scrollbar represents.
void	computeScroll() Called by a parent to request that a child update its values for mScrollX and mScrollY if necessary.
int	computeVerticalScrollExtent() Compute the vertical extent of the vertical scrollbar's thumb within the vertical range.
int	computeVerticalScrollRange() Compute the vertical range that the vertical scrollbar represents.

void	debug(int depth) Prints information about this view in the log output, with the tag VIEW_LOG_TAG.
boolean	didTouchFocusSelect() Returns true, only while processing a touch gesture, if the initial touch down event caused focus to move to the text view and as a result its selection changed.
void	drawableHotspotChanged(float x, float y) This function is called whenever the view hotspot changes and needs to be propagated to drawables or child views managed by the view.
void	drawableStateChanged() This function is called whenever the state of the view changes in such a way that it impacts the state of drawables being shown.
void	endBatchEdit()
boolean	extractText(ExtractedTextRequest request, ExtractedText outText) If this TextView contains editable content, extract a portion of it based on the information in *request* in to *outText*.
void	findViewsWithText(ArrayList<View> outViews, CharSequence searched, int flags) Finds the Views that contain given text.
CharSequence	getAccessibilityClassName() Return the class name of this object to be used for accessibility purposes.
final int	getAutoLinkMask() Gets the autolink mask of the text.
int	getAutoSizeMaxTextSize()
int	getAutoSizeMinTextSize()
int	getAutoSizeStepGranularity()
int[]	getAutoSizeTextAvailableSizes()
int	getAutoSizeTextType() Returns the type of auto-size set for this widget.
int	getAutofillType() Describes the autofill type of this view, so an AutofillService can create the proper AutofillValue when autofilling the view.
AutofillValue	getAutofillValue() Gets the View's current autofill value.

int	getBaseline() Return the offset of the widget's text baseline from the widget's top boundary.
int	getBottomPaddingOffset() Amount by which to extend the bottom fading region.
int	getBreakStrategy() Gets the current strategy for breaking paragraphs into lines.
int	getCompoundDrawablePadding() Returns the padding between the compound drawables and the text.
ColorStateList	getCompoundDrawableTintList()
PorterDuff.Mode	getCompoundDrawableTintMode() Returns the blending mode used to apply the tint to the compound drawables, if specified.
Drawable[]	getCompoundDrawables() Returns drawables for the left, top, right, and bottom borders.
Drawable[]	getCompoundDrawablesRelative() Returns drawables for the start, top, end, and bottom borders.
int	getCompoundPaddingBottom() Returns the bottom padding of the view, plus space for the bottom Drawable if any.
int	getCompoundPaddingEnd() Returns the end padding of the view, plus space for the end Drawable if any.
int	getCompoundPaddingLeft() Returns the left padding of the view, plus space for the left Drawable if any.
int	getCompoundPaddingRight() Returns the right padding of the view, plus space for the right Drawable if any.
int	getCompoundPaddingStart() Returns the start padding of the view, plus space for the start Drawable if any.
int	getCompoundPaddingTop() Returns the top padding of the view, plus space for the top Drawable if any.
final int	getCurrentHintTextColor() Return the current color selected to paint the hint text.

final int	getCurrentTextColor() Return the current color selected for normal text.
ActionMode.Callback	getCustomInsertionActionModeCallback() Retrieves the value set in setCustomInsertionActionModeCallback(ActionMode.Callback).
ActionMode.Callback	getCustomSelectionActionModeCallback() Retrieves the value set in setCustomSelectionActionModeCallback(ActionMode.Callback).
boolean	getDefaultEditable() Subclasses override this to specify that they have a KeyListener by default even if not specifically called for in the XML options.
MovementMethod	getDefaultMovementMethod() Subclasses override this to specify a default movement method.
Editable	getEditableText() Return the text that TextView is displaying as an Editable object.
TextUtils.TruncateAt	getEllipsize() Returns where, if anywhere, words that are longer than the view is wide should be ellipsized.
CharSequence	getError() Returns the error message that was set to be displayed with setError(CharSequence), or null if no error was set or if it the error was cleared by the widget after user input.
int	getExtendedPaddingBottom() Returns the extended bottom padding of the view, including both the bottom Drawable if any and any extra space to keep more than maxLines of text from showing.
int	getExtendedPaddingTop() Returns the extended top padding of the view, including both the top Drawable if any and any extra space to keep more than maxLines of text from showing.
InputFilter[]	getFilters() Returns the current list of input filters.
void	getFocusedRect(Rect r) When a view has focus and the user navigates away from it, the next view is searched for starting from the rectangle filled in by this method.

String	getFontFeatureSettings() Returns the font feature settings.
String	getFontVariationSettings() Returns the font variation settings.
boolean	getFreezesText() Return whether this text view is including its entire text contents in frozen icicles.
int	getGravity() Returns the horizontal and vertical alignment of this TextView.
int	getHighlightColor()
CharSequence	getHint() Returns the hint that is displayed when the text of the TextView is empty.
final ColorStateList	getHintTextColors()
int	getHyphenationFrequency() Gets the current frequency of automatic hyphenation to be used when determining word breaks.
int	getImeActionId() Get the IME action ID previous set with setImeActionLabel(CharSequence, int).
CharSequence	getImeActionLabel() Get the IME action label previous set with setImeActionLabel(CharSequence, int).
LocaleList	getImeHintLocales()
int	getImeOptions() Get the type of the Input Method Editor (IME).
boolean	getIncludeFontPadding() Gets whether the TextView includes extra top and bottom padding to make room for accents that go above the normal ascent and descent.
Bundle	getInputExtras(boolean create) Retrieve the input extras currently associated with the text view, which can be viewed as well as modified.
int	getInputType() Get the type of the editable content.
int	getJustificationMode()
final KeyListener	getKeyListener() Gets the current KeyListener for the TextView.

final Layout	getLayout() Gets the Layout that is currently being used to display the text.
float	getLeftFadingEdgeStrength() Returns the strength, or intensity, of the left faded edge.
int	getLeftPaddingOffset() Amount by which to extend the left fading region.
float	getLetterSpacing() Gets the text letter-space value, which determines the spacing between characters.
int	getLineBounds(int line, Rect bounds) Return the baseline for the specified line (0...getLineCount() – 1) If bounds is not null, return the top, left, right, bottom extents of the specified line in it.
int	getLineCount() Return the number of lines of text, or 0 if the internal Layout has not been built.
int	getLineHeight() Gets the vertical distance between lines of text, in pixels.
float	getLineSpacingExtra() Gets the line spacing extra space
float	getLineSpacingMultiplier() Gets the line spacing multiplier
final ColorStateList	getLinkTextColors()
final boolean	getLinksClickable() Returns whether the movement method will automatically be set to LinkMovementMethod if setAutoLinkMask(int) has been set to nonzero and links are detected in setText(char[], int, int).
int	getMarqueeRepeatLimit() Gets the number of times the marquee animation is repeated.
int	getMaxEms() Returns the maximum width of TextView in terms of ems or −1 if the maximum width was set using setMaxWidth(int) or setWidth(int).
int	getMaxHeight() Returns the maximum height of TextView in terms of pixels or −1 if the maximum height was set using setMaxLines(int) or setLines(int).

int	getMaxLines() Returns the maximum height of TextView in terms of number of lines or −1 if the maximum height was set using setMaxHeight(int) or setHeight(int).
int	getMaxWidth() Returns the maximum width of TextView in terms of pixels or −1 if the maximum width was set using setMaxEms(int) or setEms(int).
int	getMinEms() Returns the minimum width of TextView in terms of ems or −1 if the minimum width was set using setMinWidth(int) or setWidth(int).
int	getMinHeight() Returns the minimum height of TextView in terms of pixels or −1 if the minimum height was set using setMinLines(int) or setLines(int).
int	getMinLines() Returns the minimum height of TextView in terms of number of lines or −1 if the minimum height was set using setMinHeight(int) or setHeight(int).
int	getMinWidth() Returns the minimum width of TextView in terms of pixels or −1 if the minimum width was set using setMinEms(int) or setEms(int).
final MovementMethod	getMovementMethod() Gets the MovementMethod being used for this TextView, which provides positioning, scrolling, and text selection functionality.
int	getOffsetForPosition(float x, float y) Get the character offset closest to the specified absolute position.
TextPaint	getPaint() Gets the TextPaint used for the text.
int	getPaintFlags() Gets the flags on the Paint being used to display the text.
String	getPrivateImeOptions() Get the private type of the content.

float	getRightFadingEdgeStrength() Returns the strength, or intensity, of the right faded edge.
int	getRightPaddingOffset() Amount by which to extend the right fading region.
int	getSelectionEnd() Convenience for getSelectionEnd(CharSequence).
int	getSelectionStart() Convenience for getSelectionStart(CharSequence).
int	getShadowColor() Gets the color of the shadow layer.
float	getShadowDx()
float	getShadowDy() Gets the vertical offset of the shadow layer.
float	getShadowRadius() Gets the radius of the shadow layer.
final boolean	getShowSoftInputOnFocus() Returns whether the soft input method will be made visible when this TextView gets focused.
CharSequence	getText() Return the text that TextView is displaying.
TextClassifier	getTextClassifier() Returns the TextClassifier used by this TextView.
final ColorStateList	getTextColors() Gets the text colors for the different states (normal, selected, focused) of the TextView.
Locale	getTextLocale() Get the default primary Locale of the text in this TextView.
LocaleList	getTextLocales() Get the default LocaleList of the text in this TextView.
float	getTextScaleX() Gets the extent by which text should be stretched horizontally.
float	getTextSize()
int	getTopPaddingOffset() Amount by which to extend the top fading region.
int	getTotalPaddingBottom() Returns the total bottom padding of the view, including the bottom Drawable if any, the extra space to keep more than maxLines from showing, and the vertical offset for gravity, if any.

int	getTotalPaddingEnd() Returns the total end padding of the view, including the end Drawable if any.
int	getTotalPaddingLeft() Returns the total left padding of the view, including the left Drawable if any.
int	getTotalPaddingRight() Returns the total right padding of the view, including the right Drawable if any.
int	getTotalPaddingStart() Returns the total start padding of the view, including the start Drawable if any.
int	getTotalPaddingTop() Returns the total top padding of the view, including the top Drawable if any, the extra space to keep more than maxLines from showing, and the vertical offset for gravity, if any.
final TransformationMethod	getTransformationMethod() Gets the current TransformationMethod for the TextView.
Typeface	getTypeface() Gets the current Typeface that is used to style the text.
URLSpan[]	getUrls() Returns the list of URLSpans attached to the text (by Linkify or otherwise) if any.
boolean	hasOverlappingRendering() Returns whether this View has content which overlaps.
boolean	hasSelection() Return true iff there is a selection inside this text view.
void	invalidateDrawable(Drawable drawable) Invalidates the specified Drawable.
boolean	isCursorVisible()
boolean	isInputMethodTarget() Returns whether this text view is a current input method target.
boolean	isPaddingOffsetRequired() If the View draws content inside its padding and enables fading edges, it needs to support padding offsets.
boolean	isSuggestionsEnabled() Return whether or not suggestions are enabled on this TextView.

boolean	isTextSelectable() Returns the state of the textIsSelectable flag (See setTextIsSelectable()).
void	jumpDrawablesToCurrentState() Call Drawable.jumpToCurrentState() on all Drawable objects associated with this view.
int	length() Returns the length, in characters, of the text managed by this TextView
boolean	moveCursorToVisibleOffset() Move the cursor, if needed, so that it is at an offset that is visible to the user.
void	onAttachedToWindow() This is called when the view is attached to a window.
void	onBeginBatchEdit() Called by the framework in response to a request to begin a batch of edit operations through a call to link beginBatchEdit().
boolean	onCheckIsTextEditor() Check whether the called view is a text editor, in which case it would make sense to automatically display a soft input window for it.
void	onCommitCompletion(CompletionInfo text) Called by the framework in response to a text completion from the current input method, provided by it calling InputConnection.commitCompletion().
void	onCommitCorrection(CorrectionInfo info) Called by the framework in response to a text auto-correction (such as fixing a typo using a dictionary) from the current input method, provided by it calling InputConnection.commitCorrection().
void	onConfigurationChanged(Configuration newConfig) Called when the current configuration of the resources being used by the application have changed.
void	onCreateContextMenu(ContextMenu menu) Views should implement this if the view itself is going to add items to the context menu.
int[]	onCreateDrawableState(int extraSpace)

	Generate the new Drawable state for this view.
InputConnection	onCreateInputConnection(EditorInfo outAttrs) Create a new InputConnection for an InputMethod to interact with the view.
boolean	onDragEvent(DragEvent event) Handles drag events sent by the system following a call to startDragAndDrop().
void	onDraw(Canvas canvas) Implement this to do your drawing.
void	onEditorAction(int actionCode) Called when an attached input method calls InputConnection.performEditorAction() for this text view.
void	onEndBatchEdit() Called by the framework in response to a request to end a batch of edit operations through a call to link endBatchEdit().
void	onFocusChanged(boolean focused, int direction, Rect previouslyFocusedRect) Called by the view system when the focus state of this view changes.
boolean	onGenericMotionEvent(MotionEvent event) Implement this method to handle generic motion events.
boolean	onKeyDown(int keyCode, KeyEvent event) Default implementation of KeyEvent.Callback.onKeyDown(): perform press of the view when KEYCODE_DPAD_CENTER or KEYCODE_ENTER is released, if the view is enabled and clickable.
boolean	onKeyMultiple(int keyCode, int repeatCount, KeyEvent event) Default implementation of KeyEvent.Callback.onKeyMultiple(): always returns false (doesn't handle the event).
boolean	onKeyPreIme(int keyCode, KeyEvent event) Handle a key event before it is processed by any input method associated with the view hierarchy.
boolean	onKeyShortcut(int keyCode, KeyEvent event) Called on the focused view when a key shortcut event is not handled.
boolean	onKeyUp(int keyCode, KeyEvent event) Default implementation of KeyEvent.Callback.onKeyUp():

	perform clicking of the view when KEYCODE_DPAD_CENTER, KEYCODE_ENTER or KEYCODE_SPACE is released.
void	onLayout(boolean changed, int left, int top, int right, int bottom) Called from layout when this view should assign a size and position to each of its children.
void	onMeasure(int widthMeasureSpec, int heightMeasureSpec) Measure the view and its content to determine the measured width and the measured height.
boolean	onPreDraw() Callback method to be invoked when the view tree is about to be drawn.
boolean	onPrivateIMECommand(String action, Bundle data) Called by the framework in response to a private command from the current method, provided by it calling InputConnection.performPrivateCommand().
void	onProvideAutofillStructure(ViewStructure structure, int flags) Populates a ViewStructure to fullfil an autofill request.
void	onProvideStructure(ViewStructure structure) Called when assist structure is being retrieved from a view as part of Activity.onProvideAssistData.
PointerIcon	onResolvePointerIcon(MotionEvent event, int pointerIndex) Returns the pointer icon for the motion event, or null if it doesn't specify the icon.
void	onRestoreInstanceState(Parcelable state) Hook allowing a view to re-apply a representation of its internal state that had previously been generated by onSaveInstanceState().
void	onRtlPropertiesChanged(int layoutDirection) Called when any RTL property (layout direction or text direction or text alignment) has been changed.
Parcelable	onSaveInstanceState() Hook allowing a view to generate a representation of its internal state that can later be used to create a new instance with that same state.
void	onScreenStateChanged(int screenState) This method is called whenever the state of the screen this view is attached to changes.

void	onScrollChanged(int horiz, int vert, int oldHoriz, int oldVert) This is called in response to an internal scroll in this view (i.e., the view scrolled its own contents).
void	onSelectionChanged(int selStart, int selEnd) This method is called when the selection has changed, in case any subclasses would like to know.
void	onTextChanged(CharSequence text, int start, int lengthBefore, int lengthAfter) This method is called when the text is changed, in case any subclasses would like to know.
boolean	onTextContextMenuItem(int id) Called when a context menu option for the text view is selected.
boolean	onTouchEvent(MotionEvent event) Implement this method to handle touch screen motion events.
boolean	onTrackballEvent(MotionEvent event) Implement this method to handle trackball motion events.
void	onVisibilityChanged(View changedView, int visibility) Called when the visibility of the view or an ancestor of the view has changed.
void	onWindowFocusChanged(boolean hasWindowFocus) Called when the window containing this view gains or loses focus.
boolean	performLongClick() Calls this view's OnLongClickListener, if it is defined.
void	removeTextChangedListener(TextWatcher watcher) Removes the specified TextWatcher from the list of those whose methods are called whenever this TextView's text changes.
void	setAllCaps(boolean allCaps) Sets the properties of this field to transform input to ALL CAPS display.
final void	setAutoLinkMask(int mask) Sets the autolink mask of the text.
void	setAutoSizeTextTypeUniformWithConfiguration(int autoSizeMinTextSize, int autoSizeMaxTextSize, int autoSizeStepGranularity, int unit) Specify whether this widget should automatically scale the text to try to perfectly fit within the layout bounds.

void	setAutoSizeTextTypeUniformWithPresetSizes(int[] presetSizes, int unit) Specify whether this widget should automatically scale the text to try to perfectly fit within the layout bounds.
void	setAutoSizeTextTypeWithDefaults(int autoSizeTextType) Specify whether this widget should automatically scale the text to try to perfectly fit within the layout bounds by using the default auto-size configuration.
void	setBreakStrategy(int breakStrategy) Sets the break strategy for breaking paragraphs into lines.
void	setCompoundDrawablePadding(int pad) Sets the size of the padding between the compound drawables and the text.
void	setCompoundDrawableTintList(ColorStateList tint) Applies a tint to the compound drawables.
void	setCompoundDrawableTintMode(PorterDuff.Mode tintMode) Specifies the blending mode used to apply the tint specified by setCompoundDrawableTintList(ColorStateList) to the compound drawables.
void	setCompoundDrawables(Drawable left, Drawable top, Drawable right, Drawable bottom) Sets the Drawables (if any) to appear to the left of, above, to the right of, and below the text.
void	setCompoundDrawablesRelative(Drawable start, Drawable top, Drawable end, Drawable bottom) Sets the Drawables (if any) to appear to the start of, above, to the end of, and below the text.
void	setCompoundDrawablesRelativeWithIntrinsicBounds(Drawable start, Drawable top, Drawable end, Drawable bottom) Sets the Drawables (if any) to appear to the start of, above, to the end of, and below the text.
void	setCompoundDrawablesRelativeWithIntrinsicBounds(int start, int top, int end, int bottom) Sets the Drawables (if any) to appear to the start of, above, to the end of, and below the text.
void	setCompoundDrawablesWithIntrinsicBounds(Drawable left, Drawable top, Drawable right, Drawable bottom) Sets the Drawables (if any) to appear to the left of, above, to

	the right of, and below the text.
void	setCompoundDrawablesWithIntrinsicBounds(int left, int top, int right, int bottom) Sets the Drawables (if any) to appear to the left of, above, to the right of, and below the text.
void	setCursorVisible(boolean visible) Set whether the cursor is visible.
void	setCustomInsertionActionModeCallback(ActionMode.Callback actionModeCallback) If provided, this ActionMode.Callback will be used to create the ActionMode when text insertion is initiated in this View.
void	setCustomSelectionActionModeCallback(ActionMode.Callback actionModeCallback) If provided, this ActionMode.Callback will be used to create the ActionMode when text selection is initiated in this View.
final void	setEditableFactory(Editable.Factory factory) Sets the Factory used to create new Editables.
void	setElegantTextHeight(boolean elegant) Set the TextView's elegant height metrics flag.
void	setEllipsize(TextUtils.TruncateAt where) Causes words in the text that are longer than the view's width to be ellipsized instead of broken in the middle.
void	setEms(int ems) Sets the width of the TextView to be exactly ems wide.
void	setEnabled(boolean enabled) Set the enabled state of this view.
void	setError(CharSequence error) Sets the right-hand compound drawable of the TextView to the "error" icon and sets an error message that will be displayed in a popup when the TextView has focus.
void	setError(CharSequence error, Drawable icon) Sets the right-hand compound drawable of the TextView to the specified icon and sets an error message that will be displayed in a popup when the TextView has focus.
void	setExtractedText(ExtractedText text) Apply to this text view the given extracted text, as previously returned by extractText(ExtractedTextRequest, ExtractedText).
void	setFilters(InputFilter[] filters)

	Sets the list of input filters that will be used if the buffer is Editable.
void	setFontFeatureSettings(String fontFeatureSettings) Sets font feature settings.
boolean	setFontVariationSettings(String fontVariationSettings) Sets TrueType or OpenType font variation settings.
boolean	setFrame(int l, int t, int r, int b) Assign a size and position to this view.
void	setFreezesText(boolean freezesText) Control whether this text view saves its entire text contents when freezing to an icicle, in addition to dynamic state such as cursor position.
void	setGravity(int gravity) Sets the horizontal alignment of the text and the vertical gravity that will be used when there is extra space in the TextView beyond what is required for the text itself.
void	setHeight(int pixels) Sets the height of the TextView to be exactly pixels tall.
void	setHighlightColor(int color) Sets the color used to display the selection highlight.
final void	setHint(CharSequence hint) Sets the text to be displayed when the text of the TextView is empty.
final void	setHint(int resid) Sets the text to be displayed when the text of the TextView is empty, from a resource.
final void	setHintTextColor(ColorStateList colors) Sets the color of the hint text.
final void	setHintTextColor(int color) Sets the color of the hint text for all the states (disabled, focussed, selected...) of this TextView.
void	setHorizontallyScrolling(boolean whether) Sets whether the text should be allowed to be wider than the View is.
void	setHyphenationFrequency(int hyphenationFrequency) Sets the frequency of automatic hyphenation to use when determining word breaks.

void	setImeActionLabel(CharSequence label, int actionId) Change the custom IME action associated with the text view, which will be reported to an IME with actionLabel and actionId when it has focus.
void	setImeHintLocales(LocaleList hintLocales) Change "hint" locales associated with the text view, which will be reported to an IME with hintLocales when it has focus.
void	setImeOptions(int imeOptions) Change the editor type integer associated with the text view, which is reported to an Input Method Editor (IME) with imeOptions when it has focus.
void	setIncludeFontPadding(boolean includepad) Set whether the TextView includes extra top and bottom padding to make room for accents that go above the normal ascent and descent.
void	setInputExtras(int xmlResId) Set the extra input data of the text, which is the TextBoxAttribute.extras Bundle that will be filled in when creating an input connection.
void	setInputType(int type) Set the type of the content with a constant as defined for inputType.
void	setJustificationMode(int justificationMode) Set justification mode.
void	setKeyListener(KeyListener input) Sets the key listener to be used with this TextView.
void	setLetterSpacing(float letterSpacing) Sets text letter-spacing in em units.
void	setLineSpacing(float add, float mult) Sets line spacing for this TextView.
void	setLines(int lines) Sets the height of the TextView to be exactly lines tall.
final void	setLinkTextColor(ColorStateList colors) Sets the color of links in the text.
final void	setLinkTextColor(int color) Sets the color of links in the text.
final void	setLinksClickable(boolean whether) Sets whether the movement method will automatically be set

	to LinkMovementMethod if setAutoLinkMask(int) has been set to nonzero and links are detected in setText(char[], int, int).
void	setMarqueeRepeatLimit(int marqueeLimit) Sets how many times to repeat the marquee animation.
void	setMaxEms(int maxEms) Sets the width of the TextView to be at most maxEms wide.
void	setMaxHeight(int maxPixels) Sets the height of the TextView to be at most maxPixels tall.
void	setMaxLines(int maxLines) Sets the height of the TextView to be at most maxLines tall.
void	setMaxWidth(int maxPixels) Sets the width of the TextView to be at most maxPixels wide.
void	setMinEms(int minEms) Sets the width of the TextView to be at least minEms wide.
void	setMinHeight(int minPixels) Sets the height of the TextView to be at least minPixels tall.
void	setMinLines(int minLines) Sets the height of the TextView to be at least minLines tall.
void	setMinWidth(int minPixels) Sets the width of the TextView to be at least minPixels wide.
final void	setMovementMethod(MovementMethod movement) Sets the MovementMethod for handling arrow key movement for this TextView.
void	setOnEditorActionListener(TextView.OnEditorActionListener l) Set a special listener to be called when an action is performed on the text view.
void	setPadding(int left, int top, int right, int bottom) Sets the padding.
void	setPaddingRelative(int start, int top, int end, int bottom) Sets the relative padding.
void	setPaintFlags(int flags) Sets flags on the Paint being used to display the text and reflows the text if they are different from the old flags.
void	setPrivateImeOptions(String type) Set the private content type of the text, which is the EditorInfo.privateImeOptions field that will be filled in when creating an input connection.
void	setRawInputType(int type)

	Directly change the content type integer of the text view, without modifying any other state.
void	setScroller(Scroller s) Sets the Scroller used for producing a scrolling animation
void	setSelectAllOnFocus(boolean selectAllOnFocus) Set the TextView so that when it takes focus, all the text is selected.
void	setSelected(boolean selected) Changes the selection state of this view.
void	setShadowLayer(float radius, float dx, float dy, int color) Gives the text a shadow of the specified blur radius and color, the specified distance from its drawn position.
final void	setShowSoftInputOnFocus(boolean show) Sets whether the soft input method will be made visible when this TextView gets focused.
void	setSingleLine(boolean singleLine) If true, sets the properties of this field (number of lines, horizontally scrolling, transformation method) to be for a single-line input; if false, restores these to the default conditions.
void	setSingleLine() Sets the properties of this field (lines, horizontally scrolling, transformation method) to be for a single-line input.
final void	setSpannableFactory(Spannable.Factory factory) Sets the Factory used to create new Spannables.
final void	setText(int resid) Sets the text to be displayed using a string resource identifier.
final void	setText(CharSequence text) Sets the text to be displayed.
void	setText(CharSequence text, TextView.BufferType type) Sets the text to be displayed and the TextView.BufferType.
final void	setText(int resid, TextView.BufferType type) Sets the text to be displayed using a string resource identifier and the TextView.BufferType.
final void	setText(char[] text, int start, int len) Sets the TextView to display the specified slice of the specified char array.

void	setTextAppearance(Context context, int resId) *This method was deprecated in API level 23. Use setTextAppearance(int) instead.*
void	setTextAppearance(int resId) Sets the text appearance from the specified style resource.
void	setTextClassifier(TextClassifier textClassifier) Sets the TextClassifier for this TextView.
void	setTextColor(int color) Sets the text color for all the states (normal, selected, focused) to be this color.
void	setTextColor(ColorStateList colors) Sets the text color.
void	setTextIsSelectable(boolean selectable) Sets whether the content of this view is selectable by the user.
final void	setTextKeepState(CharSequence text) Sets the text to be displayed but retains the cursor position.
final void	setTextKeepState(CharSequence text, TextView.BufferType type) Sets the text to be displayed and the TextView.BufferType but retains the cursor position.
void	setTextLocale(Locale locale) Set the default Locale of the text in this TextView to a one-member LocaleList containing just the given Locale.
void	setTextLocales(LocaleList locales) Set the default LocaleList of the text in this TextView to the given value.
void	setTextScaleX(float size) Sets the horizontal scale factor for text.
void	setTextSize(int unit, float size) Set the default text size to a given unit and value.
void	setTextSize(float size) Set the default text size to the given value, interpreted as "scaled pixel" units.
final void	setTransformationMethod(TransformationMethod method) Sets the transformation that is applied to the text that this TextView is displaying.
void	setTypeface(Typeface tf) Sets the typeface and style in which the text should be displayed.

void	setTypeface(Typeface tf, int style) Sets the typeface and style in which the text should be displayed, and turns on the fake bold and italic bits in the Paint if the Typeface that you provided does not have all the bits in the style that you specified.
void	setWidth(int pixels) Sets the width of the TextView to be exactly pixels wide.
boolean	showContextMenu() Shows the context menu for this view.
boolean	showContextMenu(float x, float y) Shows the context menu for this view anchored to the specified view-relative coordinate.
boolean	verifyDrawable(Drawable who) If your view subclass is displaying its own Drawable objects, it should override this function and return true for any Drawable it is displaying.

[부록 C] MediaPlayer Class SDK 설명서

(https://developer.android.com/reference/android/media/MediaPlayer.html)

Nested classes	
class	MediaPlayer.DrmInfo Encapsulates the DRM properties of the source.
class	MediaPlayer.MetricsConstants
class	MediaPlayer.NoDrmSchemeException Thrown when a DRM method is called before preparing a DRM scheme through prepareDrm().
interface	MediaPlayer.OnBufferingUpdateListener Interface definition of a callback to be invoked indicating buffering status of a media resource being streamed over the network.
interface	MediaPlayer.OnCompletionListener Interface definition for a callback to be invoked when playback of a media source has completed.
interface	MediaPlayer.OnDrmConfigHelper Interface definition of a callback to be invoked when the app can do DRM configuration (get/set properties) before the session is opened.
interface	MediaPlayer.OnDrmInfoListener Interface definition of a callback to be invoked when the DRM info becomes available
interface	MediaPlayer.OnDrmPreparedListener Interface definition of a callback to notify the app when the DRM is ready for key request/response
interface	MediaPlayer.OnErrorListener Interface definition of a callback to be invoked when there has been an error during an asynchronous operation (other errors will throw exceptions at method call time).
interface	MediaPlayer.OnInfoListener Interface definition of a callback to be invoked to communicate some info and/or warning about the media or its playback.
interface	MediaPlayer.OnPreparedListener Interface definition for a callback to be invoked when the media source is ready for playback.

interface	MediaPlayer.OnSeekCompleteListener Interface definition of a callback to be invoked indicating the completion of a seek operation.
interface	MediaPlayer.OnTimedMetaDataAvailableListener Interface definition of a callback to be invoked when a track has timed metadata available.
interface	MediaPlayer.OnTimedTextListener Interface definition of a callback to be invoked when a timed text is available for display.
interface	MediaPlayer.OnVideoSizeChangedListener Interface definition of a callback to be invoked when the video size is first known or updated
class	MediaPlayer.ProvisioningNetworkErrorException Thrown when the device requires DRM provisioning but the provisioning attempt has failed due to a network error (Internet reachability, timeout, etc.).
class	MediaPlayer.ProvisioningServerErrorException Thrown when the device requires DRM provisioning but the provisioning attempt has failed due to the provisioning server denying the request.
class	MediaPlayer.TrackInfo Class for MediaPlayer to return each audio/video/subtitle track's metadata.

Constants	
int	MEDIA_ERROR_IO File or network related operation errors.
int	MEDIA_ERROR_MALFORMED Bitstream is not conforming to the related coding standard or file spec.
int	MEDIA_ERROR_NOT_VALID_FOR_PROGRESSIVE_PLAYBACK The video is streamed and its container is not valid for progressive playback i.e the video's index (e.g moov atom) is not at the start of the file.
int	MEDIA_ERROR_SERVER_DIED Media server died.

int	MEDIA_ERROR_TIMED_OUT Some operation takes too long to complete, usually more than 3-5 seconds.
int	MEDIA_ERROR_UNKNOWN Unspecified media player error.
int	MEDIA_ERROR_UNSUPPORTED Bitstream is conforming to the related coding standard or file spec, but the media framework does not support the feature.
int	MEDIA_INFO_AUDIO_NOT_PLAYING Informs that audio is not playing.
int	MEDIA_INFO_BAD_INTERLEAVING Bad interleaving means that a media has been improperly interleaved or not interleaved at all, e.g has all the video samples first then all the audio ones.
int	MEDIA_INFO_BUFFERING_END MediaPlayer is resuming playback after filling buffers.
int	MEDIA_INFO_BUFFERING_START MediaPlayer is temporarily pausing playback internally in order to buffer more data.
int	MEDIA_INFO_METADATA_UPDATE A new set of metadata is available.
int	MEDIA_INFO_NOT_SEEKABLE The media cannot be seeked (e.g live stream)
int	MEDIA_INFO_SUBTITLE_TIMED_OUT Reading the subtitle track takes too long.
int	MEDIA_INFO_UNKNOWN Unspecified media player info.
int	MEDIA_INFO_UNSUPPORTED_SUBTITLE Subtitle track was not supported by the media framework.
int	MEDIA_INFO_VIDEO_NOT_PLAYING Informs that video is not playing.
int	MEDIA_INFO_VIDEO_RENDERING_START The player just pushed the very first video frame for rendering.
int	MEDIA_INFO_VIDEO_TRACK_LAGGING The video is too complex for the decoder: it can't decode frames fast enough.
String	MEDIA_MIMETYPE_TEXT_SUBRIP MIME type for SubRip (SRT) container.

int	PREPARE_DRM_STATUS_PREPARATION_ERROR The DRM preparation has failed .
int	PREPARE_DRM_STATUS_PROVISIONING_NETWORK_ERROR The device required DRM provisioning but couldn't reach the provisioning server.
int	PREPARE_DRM_STATUS_PROVISIONING_SERVER_ERROR The device required DRM provisioning but the provisioning server denied the request.
int	PREPARE_DRM_STATUS_SUCCESS The status codes for onDrmPrepared(MediaPlayer, int) listener.
int	SEEK_CLOSEST This mode is used with seekTo(long, int) to move media position to a frame (not necessarily a key frame) associated with a data source that is located closest to or at the given time.
int	SEEK_CLOSEST_SYNC This mode is used with seekTo(long, int) to move media position to a sync (or key) frame associated with a data source that is located closest to (in time) or at the given time.
int	SEEK_NEXT_SYNC This mode is used with seekTo(long, int) to move media position to a sync (or key) frame associated with a data source that is located right after or at the given time.
int	SEEK_PREVIOUS_SYNC This mode is used with seekTo(long, int) to move media position to a sync (or key) frame associated with a data source that is located right before or at the given time.
int	VIDEO_SCALING_MODE_SCALE_TO_FIT Specifies a video scaling mode.
int	VIDEO_SCALING_MODE_SCALE_TO_FIT_WITH_CROPPING Specifies a video scaling mode.

Fields	
protected AudioAttributes	mAttributes
protected float	mAuxEffectSendLevel
protected float	mLeftVolume
protected float	mRightVolume

Public constructors

MediaPlayer() Default constructor.	

Public methods

void	addTimedTextSource(FileDescriptor fd, String mimeType) Adds an external timed text source file (FileDescriptor).
void	addTimedTextSource(String path, String mimeType) Adds an external timed text source file.
void	addTimedTextSource(FileDescriptor fd, long offset, long length, String mime) Adds an external timed text file (FileDescriptor).
void	addTimedTextSource(Context context, Uri uri, String mimeType) Adds an external timed text source file (Uri).
void	attachAuxEffect(int effectId) Attaches an auxiliary effect to the player.
static MediaPlayer	create(Context context, Uri uri, SurfaceHolder holder, AudioAttributes audioAttributes, int audioSessionId) Same factory method as create(Context, Uri, SurfaceHolder) but that lets you specify the audio attributes and session ID to be used by the new MediaPlayer instance.
static MediaPlayer	create(Context context, int resid, AudioAttributes audioAttributes, int audioSessionId) Same factory method as create(Context, int) but that lets you specify the audio attributes and session ID to be used by the new MediaPlayer instance.
static MediaPlayer	create(Context context, Uri uri, SurfaceHolder holder) Convenience method to create a MediaPlayer for a given Uri.
static MediaPlayer	create(Context context, int resid) Convenience method to create a MediaPlayer for a given resource id.
static MediaPlayer	create(Context context, Uri uri) Convenience method to create a MediaPlayer for a given Uri.
VolumeShaper	createVolumeShaper(VolumeShaper.Configuration configuration)

	Returns a VolumeShaper object that can be used modify the volume envelope of the player or track.
static void	deprecateStreamTypeForPlayback(int streamType, String className, String opName) Use to generate warning or exception in legacy code paths that allowed passing stream types to qualify audio playback.
void	deselectTrack(int index) Deselect a track.
int	getAudioSessionId() Returns the audio session ID.
int	getCurrentPosition() Gets the current playback position.
MediaPlayer.DrmInfo	getDrmInfo() Retrieves the DRM Info associated with the current source
String	getDrmPropertyString(String propertyName) Read a DRM engine plugin String property value, given the property name string.
int	getDuration() Gets the duration of the file.
MediaDrm.KeyRequest	getKeyRequest(byte[] keySetId, byte[] initData, String mimeType, int keyType, Map<String, String> optionalParameters) A key request/response exchange occurs between the app and a license server to obtain or release keys used to decrypt encrypted content.
PersistableBundle	getMetrics() Return Metrics data about the current player.
PlaybackParams	getPlaybackParams() Gets the playback params, containing the current playback rate.
int	getSelectedTrack(int trackType) Returns the index of the audio, video, or subtitle track currently selected for playback, The return value is an index into the array returned by getTrackInfo(), and can be used in calls to selectTrack(int) or deselectTrack(int).
SyncParams	getSyncParams() Gets the A/V sync mode.

MediaTimestamp	getTimestamp() Get current playback position as a MediaTimestamp.
TrackInfo[]	getTrackInfo() Returns an array of track information.
int	getVideoHeight() Returns the height of the video.
int	getVideoWidth() Returns the width of the video.
boolean	isLooping() Checks whether the MediaPlayer is looping or non-looping.
boolean	isPlaying() Checks whether the MediaPlayer is playing.
void	pause() Pauses playback.
void	prepare() Prepares the player for playback, synchronously.
void	prepareAsync() Prepares the player for playback, asynchronously.
void	prepareDrm(UUID uuid) Prepares the DRM for the current source If OnDrmConfigHelper is registered, it will be called during preparation to allow configuration of the DRM properties before opening the DRM session.
byte[]	provideKeyResponse(byte[] keySetId, byte[] response) A key response is received from the license server by the app, then it is provided to the DRM engine plugin using provideKeyResponse.
void	release() Releases resources associated with this MediaPlayer object.
void	releaseDrm() Releases the DRM session The player has to have an active DRM session and be in stopped, or prepared state before this call is made.
void	reset() Resets the MediaPlayer to its uninitialized state.
void	restoreKeys(byte[] keySetId) Restore persisted offline keys into a new session.

void	seekTo(int msec) Seeks to specified time position.
void	seekTo(long msec, int mode) Moves the media to specified time position by considering the given mode.
void	selectTrack(int index) Selects a track.
void	setAudioAttributes(AudioAttributes attributes) Sets the audio attributes for this MediaPlayer.
void	setAudioSessionId(int sessionId) Sets the audio session ID.
void	setAudioStreamType(int streamtype) *This method was deprecated in API level 26. use setAudioAttributes(AudioAttributes)*
void	setAuxEffectSendLevel(float level) Sets the send level of the player to the attached auxiliary effect.
void	setDataSource(AssetFileDescriptor afd) Sets the data source (AssetFileDescriptor) to use.
void	setDataSource(FileDescriptor fd) Sets the data source (FileDescriptor) to use.
void	setDataSource(FileDescriptor fd, long offset, long length) Sets the data source (FileDescriptor) to use.
void	setDataSource(String path) Sets the data source (file-path or http/rtsp URL) to use.
void	setDataSource(Context context, Uri uri, Map<String, String> headers, List<HttpCookie> cookies) Sets the data source as a content Uri.
void	setDataSource(Context context, Uri uri, Map<String, String> headers) Sets the data source as a content Uri.
void	setDataSource(MediaDataSource dataSource) Sets the data source (MediaDataSource) to use.
void	setDataSource(Context context, Uri uri) Sets the data source as a content Uri.
void	setDisplay(SurfaceHolder sh) Sets the SurfaceHolder to use for displaying the video portion of the media.

void	setDrmPropertyString(String propertyName, String value) Set a DRM engine plugin String property value.
void	setLooping(boolean looping) Sets the player to be looping or non-looping.
void	setNextMediaPlayer(MediaPlayer next) Set the MediaPlayer to start when this MediaPlayer finishes playback (i.e.
void	setOnBufferingUpdateListener(MediaPlayer.OnBufferingUpdateListener listener) Register a callback to be invoked when the status of a network stream's buffer has changed.
void	setOnCompletionListener(MediaPlayer.OnCompletionListener listener) Register a callback to be invoked when the end of a media source has been reached during playback.
void	setOnDrmConfigHelper(MediaPlayer.OnDrmConfigHelper listener) Register a callback to be invoked for configuration of the DRM object before the session is created.
void	setOnDrmInfoListener(MediaPlayer.OnDrmInfoListener listener) Register a callback to be invoked when the DRM info is known.
void	setOnDrmInfoListener(MediaPlayer.OnDrmInfoListener listener, Handler handler) Register a callback to be invoked when the DRM info is known.
void	setOnDrmPreparedListener(MediaPlayer.OnDrmPreparedListener listener, Handler handler) Register a callback to be invoked when the DRM object is prepared.
void	setOnDrmPreparedListener(MediaPlayer.OnDrmPreparedListener listener) Register a callback to be invoked when the DRM object is prepared.
void	setOnErrorListener(MediaPlayer.OnErrorListener listener) Register a callback to be invoked when an error has happened during an asynchronous operation.

void	setOnInfoListener(MediaPlayer.OnInfoListener listener) Register a callback to be invoked when an info/warning is available.
void	setOnPreparedListener(MediaPlayer.OnPreparedListener listener) Register a callback to be invoked when the media source is ready for playback.
void	setOnSeekCompleteListener(MediaPlayer.OnSeekComplete Listener listener) Register a callback to be invoked when a seek operation has been completed.
void	setOnTimedMetaDataAvailableListener(MediaPlayer.OnTime dMetaDataAvailableListener listener) Register a callback to be invoked when a selected track has timed metadata available.
void	setOnTimedTextListener(MediaPlayer.OnTimedTextListener listener) Register a callback to be invoked when a timed text is available for display.
void	setOnVideoSizeChangedListener(MediaPlayer.OnVideoSize ChangedListener listener) Register a callback to be invoked when the video size is known or updated.
void	setPlaybackParams(PlaybackParams params) Sets playback rate using PlaybackParams.
void	setScreenOnWhilePlaying(boolean screenOn) Control whether we should use the attached SurfaceHolder to keep the screen on while video playback is occurring.
void	setSurface(Surface surface) Sets the Surface to be used as the sink for the video portion of the media.
void	setSyncParams(SyncParams params) Sets A/V sync mode.
void	setVideoScalingMode(int mode) Sets video scaling mode.
void	setVolume(float leftVolume, float rightVolume) Sets the volume on this player.

void	setWakeMode(Context context, int mode) Set the low-level power management behavior for this MediaPlayer.
void	start() Starts or resumes playback.
void	stop() Stops playback after playback has been started or paused.

Protected methods	
void	baseRegisterPlayer() Call from derived class when instantiation / initialization is successful
void	finalize() Called by the garbage collector on an object when garbage collection determines that there are no more references to the object.
int	getStartDelayMs()

[부록 D] SQLiteDatabase 클래스 SDK 설명서

(https://developer.android.com/reference/android/database/sqlite/

SQLiteDatabase.html)

Nested classes	
interface	SQLiteDatabase.CursorFactory Used to allow returning sub-classes of Cursor when calling query.
class	SQLiteDatabase.OpenParams Wrapper for configuration parameters that are used for opening SQLiteDatabase

Constants	
int	CONFLICT_ABORT When a constraint violation occurs,no ROLLBACK is executed so changes from prior commands within the same transaction are preserved.
int	CONFLICT_FAIL When a constraint violation occurs, the command aborts with a return code SQLITE_CONSTRAINT.
int	CONFLICT_IGNORE When a constraint violation occurs, the one row that contains the constraint violation is not inserted or changed.
int	CONFLICT_NONE Use the following when no conflict action is specified.
int	CONFLICT_REPLACE When a UNIQUE constraint violation occurs, the pre-existing rows that are causing the constraint violation are removed prior to inserting or updating the current row.
int	CONFLICT_ROLLBACK When a constraint violation occurs, an immediate ROLLBACK occurs, thus ending the current transaction, and the command aborts with a return code of SQLITE_CONSTRAINT.

int	CREATE_IF_NECESSARY Open flag: Flag for openDatabase(File, SQLiteDatabase.OpenParams) to create the database file if it does not already exist.
int	ENABLE_WRITE_AHEAD_LOGGING Open flag: Flag for openDatabase(File, SQLiteDatabase.OpenParams) to open the database file with write-ahead logging enabled by default.
int	MAX_SQL_CACHE_SIZE Absolute max value that can be set by setMaxSqlCacheSize(int).
int	NO_LOCALIZED_COLLATORS Open flag: Flag for openDatabase(File, SQLiteDatabase.OpenParams) to open the database without support for localized collators.
int	OPEN_READONLY Open flag: Flag for openDatabase(File, SQLiteDatabase.OpenParams) to open the database for reading only.
int	OPEN_READWRITE Open flag: Flag for openDatabase(File, SQLiteDatabase.OpenParams) to open the database for reading and writing. If the disk is full, this may fail even before you actually write anything.
int	SQLITE_MAX_LIKE_PATTERN_LENGTH Maximum Length Of A LIKE Or GLOB Pattern The pattern matching algorithm used in the default LIKE and GLOB implementation of SQLite can exhibit $O(N^2)$ performance (where N is the number of characters in the pattern) for certain pathological cases.

Public methods	
void	beginTransaction() Begins a transaction in EXCLUSIVE mode.
void	beginTransactionNonExclusive() Begins a transaction in IMMEDIATE mode.
void	beginTransactionWithListener(SQLiteTransactionListener transactionListener) Begins a transaction in EXCLUSIVE mode.
void	beginTransactionWithListenerNonExclusive(SQLiteTransactionListener transactionListener) Begins a transaction in IMMEDIATE mode.

SQLiteStatement	compileStatement(String sql) Compiles an SQL statement into a reusable pre-compiled statement object.
static SQLiteDatabase	create(SQLiteDatabase.CursorFactory factory) Create a memory backed SQLite database.
static SQLiteDatabase	createInMemory(SQLiteDatabase.OpenParams openParams) Create a memory backed SQLite database.
int	delete(String table, String whereClause, String[] whereArgs) Convenience method for deleting rows in the database.
static boolean	deleteDatabase(File file) Deletes a database including its journal file and other auxiliary files that may have been created by the database engine.
void	disableWriteAheadLogging() This method disables the features enabled by enableWriteAheadLogging().
boolean	enableWriteAheadLogging() This method enables parallel execution of queries from multiple threads on the same database.
void	endTransaction() End a transaction.
void	execSQL(String sql) Execute a single SQL statement that is NOT a SELECT or any other SQL statement that returns data.
void	execSQL(String sql, Object[] bindArgs) Execute a single SQL statement that is NOT a SELECT/INSERT/UPDATE/DELETE.
static String	findEditTable(String tables) Finds the name of the first table, which is editable.
List<Pair<String, String>>	getAttachedDbs() Returns list of full pathnames of all attached databases including the main database by executing 'pragma database_list' on the database.
long	getMaximumSize() Returns the maximum size the database may grow to.
long	getPageSize() Returns the current database page size, in bytes.
final String	getPath() Gets the path to the database file.

Map<String, String>	getSyncedTables() *This method was deprecated in API level 11. This method no longer serves any useful purpose and has been deprecated.*
int	getVersion() Gets the database version.
boolean	inTransaction() Returns true if the current thread has a transaction pending.
long	insert(String table, String nullColumnHack, ContentValues values) Convenience method for inserting a row into the database.
long	insertOrThrow(String table, String nullColumnHack, ContentValues values) Convenience method for inserting a row into the database.
long	insertWithOnConflict(String table, String nullColumnHack, ContentValues initialValues, int conflictAlgorithm) General method for inserting a row into the database.
boolean	isDatabaseIntegrityOk() Runs 'pragma integrity_check' on the given database (and all the attached databases) and returns true if the given database (and all its attached databases) pass integrity_check, false otherwise.
boolean	isDbLockedByCurrentThread() Returns true if the current thread is holding an active connection to the database.
boolean	isDbLockedByOtherThreads() *This method was deprecated in API level 16. Always returns false. Do not use this method.*
boolean	isOpen() Returns true if the database is currently open.
boolean	isReadOnly() Returns true if the database is opened as read only.
boolean	isWriteAheadLoggingEnabled() Returns true if write-ahead logging has been enabled for this database.
void	markTableSyncable(String table, String deletedTable) *This method was deprecated in API level 11. This method no longer serves any useful purpose and has been deprecated.*

void	markTableSyncable(String table, String foreignKey, String updateTable) *This method was deprecated in API level 11. This method no longer serves any useful purpose and has been deprecated.*
boolean	needUpgrade(int newVersion) Returns true if the new version code is greater than the current database version.
static SQLiteDatabase	openDatabase(String path, SQLiteDatabase.CursorFactory factory, int flags) Open the database according to the flags OPEN_READWRITE OPEN_READONLY CREATE_IF_NECESSARY and/or NO_LOCALIZED_COLLATORS.
static SQLiteDatabase	openDatabase(File path, SQLiteDatabase.OpenParams openParams) Open the database according to the specified parameters
static SQLiteDatabase	openDatabase(String path, SQLiteDatabase.CursorFactory factory, int flags, DatabaseErrorHandler errorHandler) Open the database according to the flags OPEN_READWRITE OPEN_READONLY CREATE_IF_NECESSARY and/or NO_LOCALIZED_COLLATORS.
static SQLiteDatabase	openOrCreateDatabase(File file, SQLiteDatabase.CursorFactory factory) Equivalent to openDatabase(file.getPath(), factory, CREATE_IF_NECESSARY).
static SQLiteDatabase	openOrCreateDatabase(String path, SQLiteDatabase.CursorFactory factory, DatabaseErrorHandler errorHandler) Equivalent to openDatabase(path, factory, CREATE_IF_NECESSARY, errorHandler).
static SQLiteDatabase	openOrCreateDatabase(String path, SQLiteDatabase.CursorFactory factory) Equivalent to openDatabase(path, factory, CREATE_IF_NECESSARY).
Cursor	query(boolean distinct, String table, String[] columns, String selection, String[] selectionArgs, String groupBy, String having, String orderBy, String limit) Query the given URL, returning a Cursor over the result set.
Cursor	query(String table, String[] columns, String selection, String[] selectionArgs, String groupBy, String having, String orderBy, String limit) Query the given table, returning a Cursor over the result set.

Cursor	query(boolean distinct, String table, String[] columns, String selection, String[] selectionArgs, String groupBy, String having, String orderBy, String limit, CancellationSignal cancellationSignal) Query the given URL, returning a Cursor over the result set.
Cursor	query(String table, String[] columns, String selection, String[] selectionArgs, String groupBy, String having, String orderBy) Query the given table, returning a Cursor over the result set.
Cursor	queryWithFactory(SQLiteDatabase.CursorFactory cursorFactory, boolean distinct, String table, String[] columns, String selection, String[] selectionArgs, String groupBy, String having, String orderBy, String limit, CancellationSignal cancellationSignal) Query the given URL, returning a Cursor over the result set.
Cursor	queryWithFactory(SQLiteDatabase.CursorFactory cursorFactory, boolean distinct, String table, String[] columns, String selection, String[] selectionArgs, String groupBy, String having, String orderBy, String limit) Query the given URL, returning a Cursor over the result set.
Cursor	rawQuery(String sql, String[] selectionArgs, CancellationSignal cancellationSignal) Runs the provided SQL and returns a Cursor over the result set.
Cursor	rawQuery(String sql, String[] selectionArgs) Runs the provided SQL and returns a Cursor over the result set.
Cursor	rawQueryWithFactory(SQLiteDatabase.CursorFactory cursorFactory, String sql, String[] selectionArgs, String editTable, CancellationSignal cancellationSignal) Runs the provided SQL and returns a cursor over the result set.
Cursor	rawQueryWithFactory(SQLiteDatabase.CursorFactory cursorFactory, String sql, String[] selectionArgs, String editTable) Runs the provided SQL and returns a cursor over the result set.
static int	releaseMemory() Attempts to release memory that SQLite holds but does not require to operate properly.
long	replace(String table, String nullColumnHack, ContentValues initialValues) Convenience method for replacing a row in the database.

long	replaceOrThrow(String table, String nullColumnHack, ContentValues initialValues) Convenience method for replacing a row in the database.
void	setForeignKeyConstraintsEnabled(boolean enable) Sets whether foreign key constraints are enabled for the database.
void	setLocale(Locale locale) Sets the locale for this database.
void	setLockingEnabled(boolean lockingEnabled) *This method was deprecated in API level 16. This method now does nothing. Do not use.*
void	setMaxSqlCacheSize(int cacheSize) Sets the maximum size of the prepared-statement cache for this database.
long	setMaximumSize(long numBytes) Sets the maximum size the database will grow to.
void	setPageSize(long numBytes) Sets the database page size.
void	setTransactionSuccessful() Marks the current transaction as successful.
void	setVersion(int version) Sets the database version.
String	toString() Returns a string representation of the object.
int	update(String table, ContentValues values, String whereClause, String[] whereArgs) Convenience method for updating rows in the database.
int	updateWithOnConflict(String table, ContentValues values, String whereClause, String[] whereArgs, int conflictAlgorithm) Convenience method for updating rows in the database.
void	validateSql(String sql, CancellationSignal cancellationSignal) Verifies that a SQL SELECT statement is valid by compiling it.
boolean	yieldIfContended() *This method was deprecated in API level 3. if the db is locked more than once (becuase of nested transactions) then the lock will not be yielded. Use yieldIfContendedSafely instead.*
boolean	yieldIfContendedSafely() Temporarily end the transaction to let other threads run.

boolean	yieldIfContendedSafely(long sleepAfterYieldDelay) Temporarily end the transaction to let other threads run.

Protected methods	
void	finalize() Called by the garbage collector on an object when garbage collection determines that there are no more references to the object.
void	onAllReferencesReleased() Called when the last reference to the object was released by a call to releaseReference() or close().

정민포
- 1999.03~현재 : 영산대학교 컴퓨터공학부 부교수
- 2007.03~현재 : 영산대학교 컴퓨터정보통신연구소 소장
- 2017.02~현재 : 영산대학교 S/W교육센터 센터장

조혁규
- 1997.03 ~ 2003.02 : 성심외국어대학 정보통신학부 조교수
- 2003.03 ~ 현재 : 영산대학교 컴퓨터정보공학부 부교수

〈개정판〉 비전공자를 위한 안드로이드 앱 프로그래밍

1판 1쇄 인쇄 2018년 02월 26일
1판 1쇄 발행 2018년 03월 02일
저   자 정민포·조혁규
발 행 인 이범만
발 행 처 **21세기사** (제406-00015호)
  경기도 파주시 산남로 72-16 (10882)
  Tel. 031-942-7861   Fax. 031-942-7864
  E-mail : 21cbook@naver.com
  Home-page : www.21cbook.co.kr
  ISBN 978-89-8468-738-7

정가 20,000원